UNDERSTANDING GRIEF

Helping Yourself Heal

Alan Wolfelt, Ph.D.

Director
Center for Loss & Life Transition
Fort Collins, Colorado

Brunner-Routledge
New York & London

Published by
Brunner-Routledge
29 West 35th Street
New York, NY 10001

Published in Great Britain
Brunner-Routledge
11 New Fetter Lane
London EC4P 4EE

UNDERSTANDING GRIEF
Helping Yourself Heal

Printed in the United States of America

Technical Development: Tanya Benn
                         Cynthia Long
                         Marguerite Mader
                         Sheila Sheward

Library of Congress Cataloging-in-Publication Data

Wolfelt, Alan.
    Understanding grief : helping yourself heal / Alan Wolfelt.
        p.   cm.
    Includes index.
    ISBN 1-55959-038-6
    1. Grief.   2. Bereavement--Psychological aspects.   3. Loss
(Psychology)   I. Title
BF575.G7W64   1992
155.9'37--dc 20   92-53492
                                                        CIP

LCN: 92-53492

ISBN: 1-55959-038-6

DEDICATION

This book is dedicated to the life and the memory of my friend Kara Kuhn. Her life and death have touched me deeply. Her presence was one of beauty, intelligence, humor, and loving warmth.

Kara shared her hopes and dreams with me. Kara shared her love of animals with me. Kara taught me about the preciousness of each day on this earth. She taught me to "be," not just to "do."

Kara—I miss you and think of you each day. At first I cried alot, but now when I think of you I not only find myself crying, I find myself smiling and remembering your gentle spirit and loving heart.

ACKNOWLEDGEMENTS

I am indebted to thousands of people who have trusted me enough to teach me about their personal grief experiences. Through your willingness to teach me, I have been given the honor of teaching others what I have learned.

I want to thank my trainees who participate in my workshops. They have spent hours helping me refine what I have learned and challenged me to continue to not only teach, but also to be taught.

I want to thank Bridget Hingle, my office manager and right arm. She not only typed the manuscript, but also coordinated the communications with the publisher.

A special thanks to Linda Alden and Andrea Gambill who offered editorial assistance with this book. They both helped me improve the quality of the finished product.

I must also thank my publisher who was patient with me when this book was delayed. The support and understanding has been invaluable.

And finally, I thank my wife, Susan, and my children, Megan and Christopher, who bring so much meaning, purpose, and love to my life!

PREFACE

This book flows from my own personal and professional life. I have been privileged to have thousands of bereaved people "teach me" about their grief journeys. I also have experienced how my own personal losses have changed my life forever.

Perhaps my most important learning about grief is simply that grief is not something we as human beings "get over." Instead, it is something we "live with." My hope is that this book reaches out to you as a supportive companion in your grief journey.

My purpose in the pages that follow is to provide an opportunity for you to learn about your own personal grief. I hope you find this book a "safe place" to express what you feel without fear of being judged.

I have found that *many books written about grief try to tell the reader how to think and feel.* This, however, is different in one important way: it allows you to explore *how you think and feel* right now. It does not attempt to prescribe how you *should* feel. Why? To heal, you need to embrace your own unique experiences.

I have attempted to communicate in this book an "active empathy" urging you to be the expert regarding your own experience. You see, I have discovered a central learning concept in my personal "grief work" and in my work with bereaved people. Translating this learning into words reads as follows: *I can only help people when I allow them to teach me about their unique journey into grief.*

You may consider this "helping attitude" strange. After all, as a professional counselor, am I not supposed to "treat" the person who has come to me for help? No, not really. My experience has made me aware that thinking a trained counselor like myself should have answers for grieving people serves only to ultimately complicate their experience. Traditional grief therapies tend to be controlling. The counselor is supposed to be "in charge" and to know what is best for the bereaved person. This prescriptive model, however, simply does not work effectively!

I challenge counselors who visit our Center for Loss and Life Transition in Fort Collins, Colorado, to adopt a "teach me" attitude with bereaved persons. By adopting a "teach me" attitude, we as counselors are less likely to make inappropriate interpretations or judgments of the mourner's experiences. This approach helps ensure that when a bereaved person expresses feelings, attitudes, or thoughts, we avoid a potential tendency to make evaluative reactions like, "That's right" or "That shouldn't be" or worse yet, "That's pathological."

On the other hand, if we cannot overcome this tendency to be judgmental, we will probably not permit ourselves to understand and "be taught" by bereaved persons. Consequently, I have discovered if I allow you to "teach me," I not only become more helpful to you, but I am enriched and changed in meaningful ways in my own life. If you find this book helpful, please drop me a note and let me learn from you as I have from other bereaved persons.

What Is This Wound Called Grief?

"Grief work" may be some of the hardest work you ever do. Healing in grief is not a passive event. It is an active process. Because grief is work, it calls on your emotional, physical, intellectual, and spiritual energy. You cannot skirt the outside edges of your grief; you must go directly through it.

Please do not try to embrace your grief alone. You need fellow companions who will bring you comfort and support. My experience suggests trying to do grief work alone can be overwhelming. A useful analogy is as follows:

> When you go out on a sunny day, the bright sunlight on your unprotected eyes creates stress. It makes seeing difficult. Sunglasses help filter out the harmful sunrays. Maybe you can think of the stress of your grief in just that way. If you respond to the stress of the death of someone loved alone, or without sunglasses, you may be overwhelmed. But if you accept the help of other people, just like putting on the sunglasses, your work of mourning will be accomplished more easily, and with less damage to yourself.

How to Use this Book

This book is not intended to be read all at once. I ask you to read through these pages at your own pace. Don't be hard on yourself because you seem to resist exploring certain areas to which you will be asked to give thought. Give yourself permission to move at your own pace, not someone else's. If you are using it in combination with a support group experience, you may find the reading timetable outlined in Chapter XI helpful.

I ask that you continue to think, feel, and write about your own unique grief journey. Take your time. Your energy level is probably very low right now. Your grief also may make it impossible for you to read and concentrate for any sustained periods of time.

In certain places in this book, I encourage you to write about your own experience. Perhaps you are not a natural writer and tend to resist putting pencil to paper. But I urge you to try writing your thoughts and feelings. Remember—

no one is going to judge your grammar or spelling. Writing your experiences allows you to share your grief outside yourself. And you may discover some wonderful healing properties through this writing. Actually, healing can occur from both the process of writing and the reflection on what you have written.

I use the word "bereaved" to identify people who have special needs. Right now you have special needs that need to be tended to. I hope you make use of this book as one way of helping you help yourself heal.

Alan D. Wolfelt, Ph.D.
Center for Loss and Life Transition
Fort Collins, Colorado

CONTENTS

CHAPTER **I**

THE ABILITY TO LOVE REQUIRES THE NECESSITY TO MOURN

"The act of living is different all through. Her absence is like the sky, spread all over everything."

C.S. Lewis
A Grief Observed

Someone you love has died. As C.S. Lewis implies above, the sense of loss is overwhelming. Now you are faced with the difficult, but necessary need to mourn. By definition, mourning is the outward, or public, expression of your many thoughts and feelings regarding the person who has died.

You are beginning a journey that is often frightening, painful, and sometimes lonely. No words, written or spoken, can take away the pain you feel now. I hope, however, this book will bring some comfort and encouragement as you make a commitment to help yourself heal.

Perhaps you have already heard the statement, "With time, you will feel better." The feelings of grief you experience when someone loved dies are sometimes described as "emotions that heal themselves." Yet, time alone has nothing to do with healing. To heal, you must be willing to commit to learning about and understanding the grief process.

When forced to confront the death of someone loved, you must become an active participant in your own healing. But in this culture, you are often left to your own resources at the very time those resources are the most depleted.

Another disappointing reality is that you may have little, if any, preparation for a new life as a bereaved person. In the crisis of grieving, you may even fail to give yourself permission to mourn, and you will usually not receive that permission from other people.

To heal in grief, you must first acknowledge that you are not a "patient" who needs someone to do something to make you better. As a noun, the word "patient" refers to a person with a malady who is being cared for by a professional. As an adjective, it describes someone who is complacent, passive, or long-suffering. For many people who have experienced the death of someone loved, the word encompasses both of those meanings. To rediscover continued meaning in life after the loss, avoid thinking of yourself as a "patient."

Grief is not a disease. No "quick-fix" exists for the pain you are enduring. *But I promise that if you can think, feel, and see yourself as an **"active participant"** in your healing, you will experience a renewed sense of meaning and purpose in your life.*

To be human means coming to know loss as part of your life. Many losses, or "little griefs," occur along life's path. And not all your losses are as painful as others; they do not always disconnect you from yourself. But the death of someone you have loved is likely to leave you feeling disconnected from both yourself and the outside world.

I invite you to join me as I guide you in an effort to confront your grief honestly. In the following pages, I will show you how to continue rebuilding your life in a healthy and positive direction.

TO LOVE AND TO MOURN

When someone you care about dies, your capacity to love dictates your necessity to mourn. Work with thousands of bereaved persons, combined with my personal losses, have convinced me of one thing: *you can not heal without mourning or expressing your grief outwardly.* Denying your grief, running from it, or minimizing it only seems to make it more confusing and overwhelming. To lessen your hurt, you must embrace it.

Reconciling your grief does not happen quickly. *Grief is a process, not an event.* Consequently, you must be patient with yourself. When you come to trust that pain will not last forever, it becomes tolerable. Deceiving yourself into thinking that the pain does not even exist will make it intolerable.

While grief is a powerful experience, so too is the ability to help in your own healing. In your willingness to read and participate in the activities outlined in this book, you are demonstrating your commitment to re-invest in life while never forgetting the one that you have loved.

THE FREEDOM TO MOURN

In the beautiful book, *A Grief Observed,* C.S. Lewis wrote about his experience after the death of his wife. He stated, "An odd by-product of my loss is that I'm aware of being an embarrassment to everyone I meet . . . Perhaps the bereaved ought to be isolated in special settlements like lepers." As he so appropriately teaches from this experience, society often tends to make the bereaved feel intense shame and embarrassment about feelings of grief.

Shame can be described as the feeling that something you are doing is bad. And you may feel that if you mourn, then you should be ashamed. If you are perceived as "doing well" with your grief, you are considered "strong" and "under control." The message is that the well-controlled person stays rational at all times.

Combined with this message is another one. Society erroneously implies that if you, as a bereaved person, openly express your feelings of grief, you are immature. If your feelings are fairly intense, you may be labeled "overly-emotional." If your feelings are extremely intense, you may even be referred to as "crazy" or a "pathological mourner."

As a professional grief counselor, I assure you that you are not crazy. But the societal messages surrounding grief that you may often receive are! This emotional negating and outright dismissing of the legitimate need to mourn is a serious problem that must be addressed.

In our culture, pain and feelings of loss are experiences most people try to avoid. Why? Because the role of suffering is misunderstood. Normal thoughts and feelings connected to loss are typically seen as unnecessary and inappropriate. Yet, only in gathering the courage to move toward this hurt is anyone able ultimately to heal.

In your healing process, constantly work to overcome messages like "carry on," "keep your chin up," or "just keep busy." And combined with these messages is often an unstated, but strong, belief that "You have a right not to hurt. So do whatever is necessary to avoid it." Dismiss this suggestion also. The unfortunate result is you may be encouraged to pop pills to ease the pain, avoid having a funeral, or deny any and all feelings of loss.

Naturally, if you avoid your pain, the people around you will not have to "be with" you as you experience it. This situation may be more comfortable for them, but unhealthy for you. The reality is many people will try to shield themselves from pain by trying to protect you from it. Do not let anyone do this to you.

When your personal feelings of grief are met with shame-based messages, discovering how to heal yourself becomes more difficult. If you internalize these messages encouraging repression of grief, you may even become powerless to help yourself heal at all. To think that mourning is wrong may tempt you to act as if you feel better than you really do.

Ultimately, however, if you deny your emotions, you deny the essence of life.

The tears you shed when someone loved has died are the beginning of your healing process. They are an outward expression of your grief. By allowing yourself to cry, you will find comfort and allow your grief wound to heal. Remember—to heal requires that you feel, and to feel demands that you overcome the shame-based messages that don't legitimize your need to mourn.

In a sense, helping yourself heal in grief stems from a very personal commitment of wanting to heal. I hope this book creates a safe place for you to embrace your grief experience and express it. While the death of someone loved changes your life forever, repressing or denying the pain will not make it go away. *But moving toward your pain will help you heal.*

In the following pages, I invite you to begin the journey into your personal grief in a supportive and life-enhancing manner. To do so, let's first dispel some of the common myths about grief and mourning.

6   *Understanding Grief*

COMMON MYTHS ABOUT GRIEF AND MOURNING

"Grief only becomes a tolerable and creative experience when love enables it to be shared with someone who really understands."

Simon Stephens

To heal your grief requires a little preliminary work. First you must become aware of and dispel a few common myths about grief and mourning. As you read this chapter, you may discover that some of these myths you believe in; some myths may be embraced by people around you. Don't condemn yourself or others. Simply make use of any new insights to help you accomplish your work of mourning in a healthier way.

The questions that follow each myth will help you to explore how these misconceptions may be influencing your grief. Answer each question candidly and use the response as a tool to understand your personal grief journey.

IDENTIFYING THE MYTHS

Myth # 1: Grief and mourning are the same experiences.

Myth # 2: The experiences of grief and mourning progress in predictable and orderly stages.

Myth # 3: Move away from grief, not toward it.

Myth # 4: Following the death of someone loved, the goal should be to "get over" your grief as soon as possible.

Myth # 5: Tears expressing grief are only a sign of weakness.

Myth # 1: Grief and mourning are the same experiences.

The majority of people tend to use the words "grieving" and "mourning" synonymously. An important distinction, however, exists between them. Individuals move toward healing not just by grieving, but through the process of mourning.

In your effort to help yourself heal, understanding the semantic distinctions of these commonly used terms is vitally important. Simply stated, **grief** is the composite of thoughts and feelings about a loss that you experience within yourself. In other words, *grief is the internal meaning given to the experience of bereavement.*

In contrast, **mourning** is *when you take the grief on the inside and express it outside of yourself.* Another way of defining mourning is "grief gone public" or "sharing your grief outside of yourself." Crying, talking about the person who died, or celebrating special anniversary dates of the person you loved are just a few examples of mourning.

After someone loved dies, friends may encourage you to "keep your grief to yourself." The disastrous result is that all of your thoughts and feelings are neatly bottled up inside of you. A catalyst for healing, however, can only be created when you develop the courage to mourn publicly in the presence of understanding, caring persons who will not judge you. At times, of course, you will grieve alone, but *expressing your grief outside yourself is necessary if you are to move forward in your grief journey.*

Have you been the victim of Myth # 1: Grief and mourning are the same experiences? Yes _____ No __X__ If so, how will your new awareness influence your grief journey?

I feel they go hand in hand and to recognize grief is to recognize the need for Mourning my husband.

Myth #2: The experiences of grief and mourning progress in predictable and orderly stages.

Probably you have already heard about the "stages of grief." This type of thinking about dying, grief, and mourning is appealing but inaccurate. Somehow the notion of stages helps people make sense of death, an experience that is usually not orderly or predictable. Attempts have been made to replace fear and lack of understanding with the security that everyone grieves by going through the same stages. If only it were so simple!

The concept of "stages" was popularized in 1969 with the publication of Elisabeth Kubler-Ross' landmark text, *On Death and Dying.* Kubler-Ross never intended for people to literally interpret her "stages of dying." Readers, however, have done just that, and the consequences have often been disastrous.

As a bereaved person, you will probably encounter persons who have adopted a rigid system of beliefs about what you should experience in your grief journey. And if you have internalized this myth, you may also find yourself trying to prescribe your grief experience as well. Instead of allowing yourself to be where you are, you may try to force yourself to be in another stage.

For example, the responses of disorganization, fear, guilt, and explosive emotions may or may not occur. Or regression may occur anywhere along the way and invariably overlap another part of your response. Sometimes your emotions may follow each other within a short period of time; or, at other times, two or more emotions may be present simultaneously. *Remember—do not try to determine where you should be. Just allow yourself to be naturally where you are in the process.*

Everyone mourns in different ways. Personal experience is your best teacher about where you are in the grief journey. Don't think your goal is to move through prescribed stages of grief. As you read further in this book, you will find that a major theme is understanding that your grief is unique. That word means "only one." No one ever existed exactly like you before, and no one will ever be exactly like you again. As part of the healing process, *the thoughts and feelings you will experience will be totally unique to you.*

Have you been the victim of Myth # 2: The experiences of grief and mourning progress in predictable and orderly stages? Yes _X_ No _____ If so, how will your new awareness influence your grief journey? *I realize that each person is different and even if 2 people are mourning the loss of the same loved one their journeys will be different.*

Myth #3: Move away from grief, not toward it.

Our society often encourages prematurely moving away from grief instead of toward it. The result is that too many bereaved people either grieve in isolation or attempt to run away from their grief through various means.

During ancient times, stoic philosophers encouraged their followers not to mourn, believing that self-control was the appropriate response to sorrow. Today, well-intentioned, but uninformed, relatives and friends still carry on this long-held tradition. While the outward expression of grief is a requirement for healing, to overcome society's powerful message which encourages repression can be difficult.

As a counselor, I am often asked, "How long should grief last?" This question directly relates to our culture's impatience with grief and the desire to move people away from the experience of mourning. Shortly after the death, for example, the bereaved are expected to "be back to normal."

Bereaved persons who continue to express grief outwardly are often viewed as "weak," "crazy," or "self-pitying." The subtle message is "shape up and get on with life." The reality is disturbing: far too many people view grief as something to be overcome *rather than experienced.*

These messages, unfortunately, encourage you to repress thoughts and feelings surrounding the death. By doing so, you may refuse to cry. And refusing to allow tears, suffering in silence, and "being strong" are often considered admirable behaviors. Many people have internalized society's message that mourning should be done quietly, quickly, and efficiently. Don't let this happen to you.

After the death of someone loved, you also may respond to the question "How are you?" with the benign response "I'm fine." In essence, though, you are saying to the world, "I'm not mourning." Friends, family and co-workers may encourage this stance. Why? Because they don't want to talk about the death. So if you demonstrate an absence of mourning behavior, it tends to be more socially acceptable.

This collaborative pretense about mourning, however, does not meet your needs as a bereaved person. When your grief is ignored or minimized, you will feel further isolated in your journey. Ultimately, you will experience the onset of the "Am I going crazy?" syndrome. To mask or move away from your grief creates anxiety, confusion, and depression. If you receive little or no social recognition related to your pain, you will probably begin to fear that your thoughts and feelings are abnormal.

Remember—society will often encourage you to prematurely move away from your grief. You must continually remind yourself that leaning toward the pain will facilitate the eventual healing.

Have you been a victim of Myth #3: Move away from grief, not toward it? Yes _X_ No ~~✗~~ If so, how will your new awareness influence your grief journey?

The people that really care about you understand what you are going through and also understand the need for mourning –

Myth #4: Following the death of someone loved, the goal should be to "get over" your grief as soon as possible.

You may already have heard the question, "Are you over it yet?" Or, even worse, "Well, you should be over it by now." To think that as a human being you "get over" your grief is ludicrous!

In clinical terms, the final dimension of grief is often referred to as resolution, recovery, reestablishment or reorganization. I, however, prefer to use the term **reconciliation.** It does not mean getting over your grief; it means growing through it.

Reconciliation is more expressive of what occurs as you integrate the new reality of moving forward in your life without the physical presence of the person who has died. Keep in mind that right now you may not be anywhere near reconciliation. That's okay. You are where you are and will move toward reconciliation at your own pace as you do the work of mourning.

With reconciliation, you will feel a renewed sense of energy and confidence; an ability to fully acknowledge the reality of the death; and the capacity to become re-involved with the activities of living. Also, you will come to acknowledge that pain and grief are difficult, yet necessary, parts of living.

As the experience of reconciliation gradually unfolds, you also will recognize that life will be different without the presence of the person who died. And you will realize that reconciliation is a process, not an event. Beyond an intellectual understanding, you will discover an emotional and spiritual understanding. What you have known at the "head" level will now be understood at the "heart" level: the person who you loved is dead.

The pain you feel will change from being ever-present, sharp, and stinging to an acknowledged sense of loss that gives rise to renewed meaning and purpose. The feeling of loss does not completely disappear. It softens, and the intense pangs of grief become less frequent. As you begin to make future commitments, hope for a continued life emerges. You will realize that although the person who died will never be forgotten, your own life can and will move forward.

You do not "get over" your grief. As you become willing to embrace the work of your mourning, however, you can and will become reconciled to it. Unfortunately, when the people around you think you have to "resolve" your grief, they set you up to fail.

Have you been a victim of Myth #4: Following the death of someone loved, the goal should be to "get over" your grief as soon as possible? Yes _____ No _X_ If so, how will your new awareness influence your grief journey?

Myth # 5: Tears expressing grief are only a sign of weakness.

Tears of grief are often associated with personal inadequacy and weakness. The worst thing you can do, however, is to allow this judgment to prevent yourself from crying. While your tears may result in a feeling of helplessness for friends, family, and caregivers, you must not let others stifle your need to mourn openly.

Sometimes the people who care about you may directly or indirectly try to prevent your tears out of a desire to protect you and, subsequently, themselves from pain. You may hear comments like "Tears won't bring him back," or "He wouldn't want you to cry." Yet *crying is nature's way of releasing internal tension in your body, and it allows you to communicate a need to be comforted.*

While data is still limited, researchers suggest that suppressing tears may actually increase your susceptibility to stress-related disorders. It makes sense. Crying is one of the excretory processes. In reviewing other excretory processes, such as sweating and exhaling, all involve the removal of waste products from the body. Crying may serve a similar function.

The capacity to express tears appears to allow for genuine healing. In my experience of counseling bereaved people, I have even observed changes in physical expression after crying. Not only do these individuals feel better after crying, they also seem to look better. Tension and agitation seem to flow out of their bodies. The capacity to express tears appears to allow for a genuine healing.

Be constantly aware that the expression of tears is not a sign of weakness. *Your capacity to share tears is an indication of your willingness to do the "work of mourning."*

Have you been the victim of Myth #5: Tears expressing grief are only a sign of weakness? Yes _____ No __X__ If so, how will your new awareness influence your grief journey?

FINAL THOUGHTS ABOUT THE MYTHS

Please remember that the myths about grief and mourning cited above are not all inclusive. Use the space provided below to note any other "grief myths" you have encountered since the death of someone loved. How do these myths influence your grief journey?

When surrounded by people who believe in these myths, you will probably feel a heightened sense of isolation. *If the people who are closest to you are unable to emotionally support you without judging you, seek out others who can.* Usually the ability to be supportive without judging will be found in individuals who have been on a grief journey themselves and are willing to be with you during this difficult time.

When you are surrounded by people who can distinguish the myths of grief from the realities, you can experience the healing that you deserve.

NOTES REGARDING PERSONAL GRIEF MYTHS I HAVE OBSERVED

MY GRIEF
IS UNIQUE

"At bottom every man [or woman] knows well enough that he [or she] is a unique human being, only once on this earth; and by no extraordinary chance will such a marvelously picturesque piece of diversity in unity as he [or she] is, ever be put together a second time."

Nietzche

What is perhaps the nicest thing about human beings? Everyone is different. No two people are exactly alike. As a result, your grief journey will not be the same as someone else's. Your grief is unique.

Despite what you may hear, you will do the "work of mourning" in your own special way. Be careful not to compare your experience with that of other people. Do not adopt assumptions about how long your grief should last. Just consider taking a "one-day-at-a-time" approach. Doing so allows you to mourn at your own pace.

This chapter enables you to explore some of the unique factors that will influence your personal grief. The factors cited are not intended to be an all-inclusive list. They are, however, some of the most common. Following each factor are questions to contemplate. As you write out your responses, you will discover an increased understanding of the uniqueness of your grief.

Factor #1: The Nature of the Relationship With the Person Who Died

Your relationship with the person who died is different than that individual's relationship with anyone else. For example, you may have been extremely close, or "best friends," as well as husband or wife. Perhaps you loved the person who died, but you had frequent disagreements or conflicts. Or maybe you were separated by physical distance which did not allow you to be as close as you would have liked. Whatever the circumstances, you are the best person to describe and work toward understanding your relationship with the person who died.

Think about your relationship with the person who died and then respond candidly to the following questions:

1. How attached were you to this person? Describe how this attachment was reflected in your behaviors toward each other.

    Roy & I were together 24/7 for almost 20 years. I was the nurturer and problem fixer. He was my strength and protector.

2. Were there times when you had conflicts with this person? Yes _X_ No ____ If so, describe the nature of those conflicts.

Usually about money.

3. Do you feel that you have any "unfinished business" in your relationship with this person? Yes _X_ No ____ If so, describe the nature of the "unfinished business."

His disease progressed so fast that I don't feel we said good-bye.

4. Can you recall one of the times you felt very close to this person? Yes _X_ No ____ Please describe.

One night during his illness he was very scared and we talked and slept in the same bed one final time

5. What special memories will you always have about this person?

I will always remember how he loved and enjoyed being with our grandchildren

Factor #2: Circumstances Surrounding the Death

The unique circumstances surrounding the death of someone loved can have an impact on your journey into grief. For example, was the death anticipated or sudden and unexpected? How old was the person who died? Do you feel you might have been able to prevent the death?

A sudden, unexpected death obviously does not allow you any opportunity to prepare yourself for the reality of the event. But ask yourself, "Are you ever 'ready' for that moment at all?" Note that even when you have the opportunity to anticipate a death, it does not lessen your grief.

The age of the person who died also has an impact on your psychological acceptance of the death. Within the order of the world, you usually anticipate that parents will die before their children. But when a child dies, it is an assault on the natural course of events. Or your grief might be affected when a "middle-aged" person dies when thought to be in the "prime of his or her life."

You may ask yourself if you could have done anything to have prevented the death. To assess your culpability after the death of someone loved is natural. Be aware, however, that while you may tend to blame yourself for the death, you did not cause it to happen. Sometimes, on the other hand, special circumstances are involved with the death of someone loved. For example, if you fell asleep while driving and someone else was killed. This type of situation can cause complications in your grief experience and further contribute to the uniqueness of your grief.

Write your responses to the following questions to help you better understand the unique circumstances surrounding the nature of the death.

1. How did he or she die?

    Cancer

2. How old was the person who died? ___*56*___ How does the age of the person affect your grief?

    I feel that just when he & I could start enjoying life together (after retirement) he was taken from me

3. Was the death anticipated, or was it sudden and unexpected? What influence does this factor have on your grief?

It was sudden and unexpected. We faced it as best we could but; it was too soon.

4. Do you have any sense that you should have been able to prevent the death? Yes __X__ No _____ If so, write out your thoughts and feelings about this.

I was always the problem fixer in our marriage and was helpless to fix this.

Factor #3: Circumstances Surrounding Your Support System

Mourning, as I have defined it in this book, requires the outside support of other human beings in order for you to heal. Without a stabilizing support system of at least one other person, the odds are you will have difficulty in doing this "work of mourning." *To heal requires an environment of empathy, caring, and gentle encouragement.*

Sometimes other people may suspect you have a support system when, in fact, you do not. For example, you may have family members or friends who live near you, but you discover that they have little compassion for, or lack patience with you and your grief. If so, a vital ingredient to your healing is missing.

Or you also may have some friends or relatives who are supportive for a relatively short period of time after the death. In the weeks that follow the death, however, this support drops off quickly. Again, *for healing to occur, social support must be ongoing.*

Even when you have a viable support system in place, are you able to accept the support that is available to you? If you are ashamed about your need to mourn, you may end up isolating yourself from the very people who would most like to "walk with you" in your time of grief. If you do so, you set yourself up to grieve inwardly rather than mourning outside of yourself.

Write your responses to the following questions so you will better understand the unique nature of your support system.

1. Do you have a stabilizing support system available? Yes __X__ No _____ If so, who makes up your support system for understanding your need to mourn?

Son & daughter-in-law
daughter
Brother & wife
niece
sister
Counselor
grief group

2. Are there some people in your life whom you wish were supportive, but who are not? Yes _X_ No _~~x~~_ If so, who are these people?

   neighbors

3. Why is it difficult for them to "be with you" in your grief?

   Not real close to them.

4. Does physical distance from people influence your support system? Yes _____ No _X_ Explain.

5. Are you able to accept support from people who want to be helpful? Yes __✗__ No _____ If not, why are you unable to accept support?

Factor #4: Your Unique Personality

Your unique personality will be reflected in your grief. For example, if you are quiet by nature, you may express your grief quietly. If you are outgoing, you may be more expressive with your grief.

Your responses to other losses or crises in your life will also probably be consistent with how you respond to the death of someone loved. If you like to remain distant or run away from crises, you may do the same thing now. If you, however, have always confronted crises head-on and openly expressed your thoughts and feelings, you may now follow that pattern of behavior.

Other personality influences, such as your self-esteem, values, and beliefs, also impact your response to the death. In addition, any long-term problems with depression or anxiety may influence your response at this time.

Write your responses to the following questions so you will better understand how unique factors in your personality influence your grief journey.

1. What are some adjectives you would use to describe yourself?

    outgoing
    sensitive to others feelings
    nurturess

2. How is your unique personality influencing your journey into grief?

    I have no one to nurture and care for. Thus a feeling of abandonment

3. How have you responded to previous losses or crises in your life?

    I had Roy for support when my son was killed and when my granddaughter died. I could lean on his strength.

4. Are you responding in a similar way now, or does it seem different than in the past? Explain.

Its different because I'm basically alone in my grief. I can't lean on Roy.

5. What has your self-esteem been like over the years?

I have always been self-assured and my self-esteem has been good.

6. How is your self-esteem right now?

Its shaky and I feel useless and not needed.

7. Have you had previous concerns with long-term depression or anxiety in your life? Yes _____ No X_____ If so, how might this influence your response to this death?

Factor #5: The Unique Personality of the Person Who Died

Just as your own personality is reflected in your grief journey, so, too, is the personality of the person who died. For example, if that person was always a soothing, stabilizing influence within the family, your family may not be as close as prior to the death. In contrast, if the person who died was never easy to be around, you may find yourself experiencing ambivalent feelings about the loss. Whatever your feelings are, talk about them openly. *The key is finding someone you can trust who will not judge your feelings.*

Respond to the following questions so you can better understand how the unique personality of the person who died influences your grief journey.

1. What was the personality like of the person who died?

He was quiet and a loner. He would have been happy if we could have lived on an island or a Mountain retreat

2. What are some adjectives you would use to describe this person?

difficult sometimes
quiet

3. What roles did the person play in your life (for example, best friend, competitor, stabilizer, mentor, disrupter, lover) and how was this role influenced by his or her personality?

best friend
lover
soulmate

4. What personality traits did this person have that you enjoyed the most in your relationship?

A quiet but strong stability

5. If you can recall, give an example of a specific time when these positive traits were expressed by this person?

6. What personality traits did this person have that you did not always care for in your relationship?

7. Do you remember an example of a specific time when these negative traits were expressed by this person? Yes _____ No _____ If so, please describe below.

Factor #6: Your Own Cultural Background

Cultural influences can be an important influence on how you express your grief. Your family probably had cultural traditions that were passed down through the generations. For example, families with German heritage sometimes demonstrate a more stoic, stiff upper lip approach to loss. An Italian family might be more expressive with feelings. While you may not be consciously aware of these cultural influences, taking time to explore these questions might create some new awareness for you.

Respond to the following questions so you will better understand how your cultural background influences your grief journey.

1. What is your cultural background?

\

2. Does this background influence your mourning? Yes _____ No _____ If so, how?

3. Does this cultural background help or hinder you in your "work of mourning?" Yes _____ No _____ Please explain.

Factor #7: Your Religious or Spiritual Background

Your personal belief system can have a tremendous impact on your journey into grief. You may discover that your religious or spiritual life is deepened, renewed, or changed as a result of your loss. Or you may well find yourself questioning your previously held belief system as part of your work of mourning.

When someone loved dies, some people may feel very close to God or a Higher Power, while others may feel more distant and hostile. You may find yourself asking questions like "Why has this happened to me?" or "What is the meaning of this experience?" You may, however, not find the answers to the multitude of questions related to your faith or spirituality.

Mistakenly, people may think that with faith, there is no need to mourn. If you support this premise, you will set yourself up to grieve internally, but not mourn externally. *Having faith does not mean you do not need to mourn. It does mean having the courage to allow yourself to mourn.*

With the death of someone you love comes a "search for meaning." You will find yourself reevaluating your life based on this loss. You will need someone who is willing to listen to you as you explore your religious or spiritual values, question your attitude toward life, and renew your resources for living. This process takes time, and it can lead to possible changes in your values, beliefs, and life-style. The questions below will hopefully provide you with a framework to explore where you are right now in your religious or spiritual life.

Respond to the following questions to better understand how your religious and spiritual beliefs influence your grief journey.

1. What are the religious or spiritual teachings with which you grew up?

2. What is your current religious, spiritual, or philosophical belief system as it relates to life and death?

3. How has this death impacted your belief system?

4. Do you have any "Why?" questions right now?
   Yes _____ No _____ If so, what are they?

5. Do you have a support system of people around you
   to validate your belief system? Yes _____ No _____ If
   so, identify this support system and explore what this
   means to you right now.

6. If faith is a part of your life, do you believe that "having faith means I'm not supposed to mourn?" Yes _____ No _____ If so, explore below what you can do to free yourself from this kind of thinking.

7. How do you see your religious or spiritual belief system playing a part in your healing process? Yes _____ No _____ Please explain.

Factor #8: Other Crises or Stresses in Your Life

The death of someone loved can often bring to the surface what are formally called "secondary losses." An individual loss seldom occurs in isolation. You may experience the loss of financial security, the loss of a sense of future, the loss of some long-time friends who abandon you in your grief, the loss of your home or perhaps the loss of your community. You also may be unemployed or experiencing strained family relationships. Take note that staying aware of how these other losses can and will influence your grief is very important.

Respond to the following questions to better understand how the other crises or stresses in your life influence your grief journey.

1. What other losses have come about in your life as a result of this death?

2. How do you see these additional losses influencing your grief?

3. What other stresses or crises are a part of your life right now?

4. How do you see these additional stresses or crises influencing your grief?

5. What can you do right now to help yourself cope with these losses or stresses?

Factor #9: Your Biological Sex

Being a male or female can have an influence not only on your grief, but also on how people relate to you at this time. While being careful not to generalize, men are often encouraged and expected to "be strong" and restrained. Typically, men have more difficulty in allowing themselves to move toward painful feelings than women do.

Women sometimes experience difficulties in expressing feelings of anger. In contrast, men tend to be more quick to respond with explosive emotions. Because men are conditioned to be totally self-sufficient, they often have difficulty accepting outside support.

1. How does your biological sex influence the expression of your grief?

2. Has your biological sex influenced how people support you in your grief?   Yes _____   No _____   If so, how?

3. Do you see any advantages or disadvantages to being the sex that you are in experiencing your grief? Yes ____ No ____ If so, what are these advantages or disadvantages?

Factor #10: The Ritual or Funeral Experience

Decisions you make relating to the funeral can either help or hinder your personal grief experience. No single, right way exists to have a funeral. We do know, however, that creating a meaningful ritual for survivors can aid in the social, emotional, and spiritual healing after a death.

A funeral helps provide an appropriate setting that permits and encourages you to express your feelings. In other words, the ritual you create legitimizes your feelings related to the loss. The funeral also can serve as a time to honor the person who has died, bring you closer to others who can give you needed support, affirm that life goes on even in the face of death, and give you a context of meaning related to your own religious, spiritual, or philosophical background.

If you were unable to attend the funeral of the person who died, or if the funeral was somehow minimized or distorted, you may find that this complicates your healing process. Be assured, however, that some things can still be done by you to help yourself heal.

What you choose to do with a funeral ritual is a very individual experience. The key is for you to feel that whatever ritual you have selected has helped meet your emotional and spiritual needs. If not, it is never too late after a death for you to plan and implement a ritual that will help meet your needs. You deserve it, and so does the person in your life who died.

Respond to the following questions to help you better understand how the funeral ritual or experience influences your grief journey.

1. Did you participate in a funeral for the person who died? Yes _____ No _____ If so, how did this help meet your needs?

2. Were you unable to participate in some kind of funeral for the person who died? Yes _____ No _____ If not, how do you feel about that?

3. Do you feel a need to create any additional ritual that would help you with your grief? Yes _____ No _____ If so, what could you do to make this happen?

4. In what ways can you continue to ritualize the death of this person such as by remembering anniversaries or other special occasions?

Other Influences on Your Grief

As noted in the introduction to this chapter, the factors that influence your grief outlined earlier in this chapter are not all inclusive. In the space provided below, note other unique influences on your grief:

CHAPTER

WHAT MIGHT
I EXPECT?

"Sometimes, when one person is missing, the whole world seems depopulated."

Lamartine

Experiencing the death of someone loved affects your head, heart and spirit. Some well-intentioned people may try to tell you exactly what, when, and how you should feel. Unfortunately, they are misinformed! Only *you* know how you feel.

Your uniqueness as a human being is reflected in your work of mourning. You may experience a variety of emotions as part of your experience. Sometimes these emotions will follow each other within a short period of time. Sometimes they will occur simultaneously. You cannot predict or prescribe what feelings may be the most intense at a particular moment.

Grief is like waves coming in from the ocean. At times, the waves are small and barely noticeable. But, when you least suspect it, a huge wave pulls your feet right out from under you. No two people ever see these waves exactly the same way, and no one reacts in the same way to each incoming wave.

As strange as your emotions may seem, they are a true expression of where you are now. They are normal and healthy. Allow yourself to learn from your feelings. Don't be surprised if you suddenly experience surges of grief, even at the most unexpected times. These grief attacks can be frightening and leave you feeling overwhelmed. They are, however, a natural response to the death of someone loved.

A vital self-care need is to familiarize yourself with thoughts, feelings, and behaviors that you may or may not experience in your grief journey. Through this awareness, you will become capable of nurturing yourself in ways that will lead to healing.

Before exploring some of your possible responses to the loss of someone loved, please take a moment to write a few words that describe how you are feeling now. In the space provided below, complete the following statement "Right now, I'm feeling . . . "

My goal for this book is to present a model of the many thoughts, feelings, and behaviors associated with grief. This model is based on my personal experiences with loss, my work with thousands of grieving people, and teachings from the literature. The ideas explored here are not all-inclusive; however, I do hope this information will help you in your grief journey. I hope this information will help you heal.

Please note that in the following pages, I have used the term *dimension* rather than *stage* of grief to reinforce the thinking that the grief experience does not occur in an orderly, predictable way.

While your grief is unique, to become aware of some of the more common dimensions of the grief experience is helpful. Questions throughout this chapter will encourage you to see if the particular dimension described is currently, or has been, a part of your personal experience. In addition, you may not have experienced a particular dimension described yet, but may find yourself doing so in the future.

SHOCK, DENIAL, NUMBNESS, DISBELIEF

Thank goodness for shock, denial, numbness, and disbelief! These feelings are nature's way of temporarily protecting you from the full reality of the death of someone loved. In reflecting on this experience, many people make comments like, "I was there, but yet I really wasn't," "It was like a dream," "I managed to do what needed to be done, but I didn't feel a part of it." You may feel dazed and stunned during this time.

In addition, when little, if any, opportunity was available to anticipate the death, this constellation of experiences is typically heightened and prolonged. Even when the death of someone loved is expected, however, you can still experience shock and disbelief.

This experience creates an insulation from the reality of the death until you are more able to tolerate what you don't want to believe. It serves as a "temporary time-out" or "psychological shock absorber." *Your emotions need time to catch up with what your mind has been told.* At one level, you know the person is dead, yet you are not able or willing to believe it.

You may not remember specific words spoken to you during the time surrounding the death of someone loved. Your mind is blocking; it is not connected to listening. Although you may not remember some, or any, of the words spoken, you may well remember if you felt comforted by the people around you. Their nonverbal presence is probably more important to you than any words they might say.

This mixture of shock, denial, numbness, and disbelief acts as an anesthetic; the pain exists, but you may not experience it in full reality. Your body, mind, and spirit take over to help you survive. Typically, a physiological component also accompanies this experience. It includes a take over by the autonomic nervous system causing heart palpitations, queasiness, stomach pain, and dizziness.

Hysterical crying, outbursts of anger, and even laughing or fainting may occur. Expressing these behaviors allows for your survival. Unfortunately, some people may try to shut-down these behaviors which actually help you survive during this time. They may try to "quiet you" in an effort to feel more comfortable within themselves. Remember—your needs are the priority right now, not theirs. Do what you need to do in order to survive.

This dimension of the grief experience typically reflects only the beginning of your grief journey. Embracing the full reality of the death cannot and should not occur quickly. You will encounter the reality of the loss only when your head, heart, and spirit are ready to.

Grief does not necessarily get easier as time passes. To tell you so would not only be untrue, but inappropriate. As you do the "work of mourning," you will have some days that are better than others. But on some days the full depth of your loss will hit you. On those days, you may not feel like getting out of bed. Keep in mind, however, *with the hurt comes healing.* At this point in the process, just remember to take "one day at a time."

Even after you have moved beyond shock, denial, numbness, and disbelief, don't be surprised if these feelings should re-emerge. Birthdays, holidays, anniversaries, or other special occasions that may only be known to you often trigger these feelings. Again, this is normal. It allows you to be where you are at this moment in time.

Your mind may approach and retreat from the reality of the death over and over again as you try to embrace and integrate the meaning of the death into your life. During your grief journey, you may even hope that you will wake up from a bad dream and discover that none of this pain happened.

Self Inventory

In the space provided, write what your experiences with shock, denial, numbness, and disbelief have been to date. If you need more space, start a personal journal that will allow you to further expand on your thoughts and feelings.

Complete the following thought: "My experience with shock, denial, numbness, disbelief is, or has been . . . "

Self-care Guidelines

A critical point to realize is that shock, denial, numbness, and disbelief are not feelings you should try to prevent yourself from experiencing. Instead, be thankful this "shock absorber" is available at a time when you need it most. Be compassionate with yourself. Allow for this instinctive form of self-protection. This dimension of grief provides a much needed, yet temporary means of survival.

A primary self-care principle is to have the availability of caring, supportive friends, family, and caregivers whom you can trust. Your instinctive response during this time is to have other people care for you. That's good because when someone loved dies, you are most unable to care for yourself. *Let yourself be nurtured.*

A few misguided people may try to "talk you out" of your denial. They will make comments like, "You just have to admit what has happened." While your ultimate healing requires acknowledging the reality of the death, this period is probably not the time to embrace the depth of your loss. Any premature effort to push the reality away can be potentially damaging to you. If someone insists on taking away your need to deny the death, avoid them.

Accepting support does not mean being totally passive and do nothing for yourself. Actually, having someone take over completely is usually not helpful. Given appropriate support and understanding, you will find value in doing for yourself. In other words, don't allow anyone to do for you what you want to do yourself.

Be kind to yourself. Feeling dazed or numb when someone loved dies is often part of your early grief experience. This numbness serves a valuable purpose: it gives your emotions time to catch up with what your mind has told you. It creates insulation from the reality of the death until you are more able to tolerate what you don't want to believe.

Personal Self-care Inventory

In the space provided, write what you are doing, or have done, to help yourself with the feelings of shock, denial, numbness, and disbelief:

DISORGANIZATION, CONFUSION, SEARCHING, YEARNING

Perhaps the most isolating and frightening part of your grief journey is the sense of disorganization, confusion, searching, and yearning that often comes with the loss. These experiences frequently come when you begin to be confronted with the reality of the death. As one bereaved person said, "I felt as if I were a lonely traveler with no companion, and worse yet, no destination. I couldn't find myself or anybody else."

This dimension of grief may cause the "going crazy syndrome." A frequently heard comment is, "I think I'm going crazy." In grief, thoughts and behaviors are different from what you normally experience. It's only natural that you may not know if your thoughts, feelings, and behaviors are normal or abnormal. The experiences described below are common after the death of someone loved. A major goal of this chapter is to simply validate these experiences so you will know you are not crazy!

After the death of someone loved, you may feel a sense of restlessness, agitation, impatience, and ongoing confusion. It's like being in the middle of a wild, rushing river where you can't get a grasp on anything. Disconnected thoughts race through your mind, and strong emotions may be overwhelming.

You may express disorganization and confusion in your inability to complete any tasks. A project may get started but go unfinished. Forgetfulness and low-work effectiveness are commonplace for many people experiencing this dimension of grief. Early morning and late at night are times when you may feel most disoriented and confused. These feelings are often accompanied by fatigue and lack of initiative. Everyday pleasures may not seem to matter anymore.

You also may experience a restless searching for the person who has died. Yearning and preoccupation with memories can leave you feeling drained. Yes, the work of mourning is draining. It often leaves you feeling wiped out.

You might even experience a shift in perception; other people may begin to look like the person in your life who died. You might be at a shopping mall, look down a hallway and think you see the person you loved so much. Or see a car go past that was like the person's who died and find yourself following the car. Sometimes you might hear the garage door open and the person entering the house as he or she had done so many times in the past. If these experiences are happening to you, remember—you are not crazy!

Visual hallucinations occur so frequently that they cannot be considered abnormal. I personally prefer the term "memory picture" to hallucination. As part of your searching and yearning when you are bereaved, you may not only experience a sense of the dead person's presence, but you also may have fleeting glimpses of the person across a room. Again, remember those words—you are not crazy!

Other common experiences during this time include difficulties with eating and sleeping. You may experience a loss of appetite, or find yourself overeating. Even when you do eat, you may be unable to taste the food. Difficulty in going to sleep and early morning awakening also are common experiences associated with this dimension of grief.

You also may dream about the person who died. Dreams can be an unconscious means of searching for this person. Be careful not to over-interpret your dreams. Simply remain open to learning from them. If the dreams are pleasant, embrace them; if they are disturbing, find someone whom you feel will understand to talk to about them.

You might find it helpful to remember that disorganization following loss always comes before any kind of reorientation. Some people will try to have you bypass any kind of disorganization or confusion. Remember—it simply cannot be done. While it may seem strange, keep in mind that your disorganization and confusion are actually stepping stones on your path toward healing.

Self Inventory

In the space provided, complete the following thought: "My experience with disorganization, confusion, searching, and yearning is or has been . . . "

Self-care Guidelines

If disorganization, confusion, searching, and yearning are, or have been, a part of your grief journey, don't worry about the normalcy of your experience. A critically important point is to never forget those reassuring words—you are not crazy!

When you feel disoriented, talk to someone who will understand. To heal, grief must be shared outside of yourself. I hope you have at least one person whom you feel understands and will not judge you. That person must be patient and attentive because you may tell your story over and over again as you work to embrace your grief. He or she must be genuinely interested in understanding you. If you are trying to talk about your disorganization and confusion, and the person doesn't want to listen, find someone who will better meet your needs.

The thoughts, feelings, and behaviors of this dimension do not come all at once. They are often experienced in a wave-like fashion. Hopefully, you will have someone to support you through each wave. You may need to talk and cry for long periods of time. At other times, you may just need to be alone. Don't try to interpret what you think and feel. Just experience it. Sometimes when you talk you may not think you make much sense. And you may not. But talking it out can still be self-clarifying at a level of experience of which you may not even be aware.

During this time, discourage yourself from making any critical decisions like selling the house and moving to another community. With the judgment-making difficulties that naturally come with this part of the grief experience, ill-timed decisions might result in more losses. Go slow and be patient with yourself.

Personal Self-care Inventory

In the space provided on the next page, write out what you are doing, or have done, to help yourself with the feelings of disorganization, confusion, searching, and yearning:

ANXIETY, PANIC, FEAR

Feelings of anxiety, panic, and fear also may be a part of your grief experience. You may ask yourself questions like, "Will my life have any purpose without this person?" "Am I going to be okay?" "Will our family survive this?" These questions are natural. Your feelings of security have been threatened; anxiety often results.

As your head and heart miss the person who was a part of your life, panic may set in. Feelings of anxiety and fear often elicit thoughts about "going crazy." If you begin to think you are "abnormal," your level of fear also may increase.

A variety of thoughts can increase your anxiety, panic, and fear. For example, you may experience fear of what the future holds; fear that one person's death will result in other deaths; increased awareness of your own mortality; feelings of vulnerability about being able to survive without the person who has died; inability to concentrate; and emotional, physical, and spiritual fatigue.

Your energy is drained, and you can easily feel overwhelmed by everyday concerns. If you add financial problems, your fear might also increase about becoming dependent on others. Obviously, anxiety, panic, and fear can be a part of the normal process of your grief journey.

Self Inventory

In the space provided, complete the following thought: "My experience with anxiety, panic, and fear is or has been . . ."

Self-care Guidelines

If anxiety, panic, and fear are a part of your grief journey you will need to talk to someone who will be understanding and supportive. Not talking about these feelings makes them grow even larger.

Review the information you just noted under your SELF INVENTORY. Find a friend or understanding counselor who is willing to explore these experiences with you. Your supportive helper can listen and be a sounding board as you express whatever you need to talk out.

Under no circumstances are you to allow your fears to go unexpressed. If you don't talk about them, you may retreat from other people and from the world in general. Many bereaved people become prisoners in their own homes. They have repressed their anxiety, panic, and fear only to discover that these feelings are now controlling them. Don't let this happen to you.

Personal Self-care Inventory

In the space provided, write what you are doing, or have done, to help yourself with the feelings of anxiety, panic, and fear:

PHYSIOLOGICAL CHANGES

Your body may be letting you know it feels distressed. Actually, one literal definition of the word "grievous" is "causing physical suffering." You may be shocked by how much your body responds to the impact of your loss. Remember—your body is naturally attuned to your stress. I will share some thoughts about how your body might react to your grief.

Among the most common physical responses to loss are trouble with sleeping and low energy. You may have difficulty getting to sleep. Perhaps even more commonly, you may wake up early in the morning and have trouble getting back to sleep. During your grief journey, your body needs more rest than usual. You may also find yourself feeling tired more quickly—sometimes even at the start of the day.

Sleeping normally after a loss would be unusual. Primarily, sleeping relates to releasing control. When someone in your life dies, you feel a loss of control. The need to stay awake sometimes relates to the fear of additional losses; therefore, you may stay awake because you want to prevent any more loss. Some bereaved people have even taught me that they stay awake hoping to not miss the person who has died if they return. If you have this experience, be assured you are not crazy. It is a normal part of searching and yearning for the person who died.

Fears of overwhelming, painful thoughts and feelings that might be expressed through dreams also may cause difficulty with sleeping. Or you also may be afraid of being alone in bed when you are not used to sleeping by yourself. Again, these are natural, but usually temporary ways, that you express your grief.

Muscle aches and pains, shortness of breath, feelings of emptiness in your stomach, tightness in your throat or chest, digestive problems, sensitivity to noise, heart palpitations, queasiness, nausea, headaches, increased allergic reactions, changes in appetite, weight loss or gain, agitation, and generalized tension—all are ways your body may react to the loss of someone loved. Any kind of chronic existing health problems may become worse. Obviously, your body will communicate about the stress you are experiencing.

Good self-care is important at this time. The stress of grief can suppress your immune system and make you more likely to experience physical problems. Right now you may not feel in control of how your body is responding. Keep in mind, however, in the majority of instances, the physical symptoms described above are normal and temporary.

Should any of these symptoms be part of your grief experience, don't be overly alarmed. The key is to take good care of your body. With proper nurturing, it will heal as you do the work of mourning. See a physician for specific physical symptoms that concern you. And, if possible, be sure to plan to get a good physical examination within the first two months after the death.

Self Inventory

In the space provided, complete the following thought: "My experience with physiological changes is or has been . . ."

Self-care Guidelines

Your body is a very sensitive instrument. When you are stressed, it responds! Your increased awareness of how your body reacts to the loss is part of the turning inward required for healing the body, mind, and spirit. You are encountering a severe blow; your body is probably letting you know it.

Practice good self-care as you experience your grief. A few reminders of good self-care include the following:

1. Get appropriate nutritional balance in your diet. If your appetite is suppressed right now, consider using a liquid meal like Instant Breakfast. Be certain to meet your daily nutritional needs.

2. Maintain appropriate fluid intake. Your thirst mechanism may be overridden when you are mourning. So be certain to drink five or six, 10 to 12 ounce glasses of water each day. Avoid caffeine; it will dehydrate you.

3. Exercise daily. Regular exercise helps you with your self-healing. A brisk 20-minute walk each day by yourself or with a close, understanding friend will help you not only physically, but emotionally and spiritually. Some of your body's discomfort can actually be relieved by some form of moderate, regular exercise.

4. Rest during the day. Watch out for people who, although well-intended, try to keep you "busy" all the time. Your body and soul need more rest now than at other times in life. And if your normal sleep pattern is impaired (or even if it isn't), you will probably find yourself feeling tired during the day. Don't think you are feeling sorry for yourself if you build in periods of rest. Many bereaved people find that building in an hour of quiet rest toward the middle of each day is helpful. If you can't sleep at night as you normally would, try to rest your body during this time. Remember—problems with sleep are normal during times of grief.

5. Schedule a general medical examination within the first two months after the death. Explore any physical symptoms with your doctor. It will rule out any potential organic diseases. Be certain, however, to see a doctor who is sensitive to your grief. Your doctor should take time to respond to your questions and help you understand your body's response to the loss. If your physical symptoms don't lessen over time, discuss your concerns with a trusted friend or counselor.

6. Be certain to "talk out" your grief. Many bereaved people have taught me if they avoid or repress talking about the death, their bodies will respond in kind. In other words, if you don't talk about your feelings, your body will try to express them for you. To ensure a forum for open communication about your feelings, a regular, stabilizing support system that allows you to share your grief must be part of your self-care plan!

Personal Self-care Inventory

In the space provided, write what you are doing, or have done, to help yourself with your body's response to your loss:

EXPLOSIVE EMOTIONS

Anger, hate, blame, terror, resentment, rage, and jealousy—all are explosive emotions that may be a volatile, yet natural, part of your grief journey. Explosive emotions relate to your survival instincts. With loss often comes the desire to protest. Explosive emotions provide the vehicle to do so.

Unfortunately, our society lacks an understanding of the normalcy of these emotions. They are, therefore, behaviors that are most often upsetting to the people around you and even to yourself. My goal is to help you understand the nature of explosive emotions. Also, I encourage you to give yourself permission to feel whatever you feel. To deny emotions, whatever they might be, is to deny the essence of life.

Some people oversimplify explosive emotions by talking only about anger. Actually, you may experience a whole range of feelings such as those listed above. Underneath these emotions are usually feelings of pain, helplessness, fear, and hurt. While each of these emotions have unique features, they are enough alike to explore them together at this point.

Some people may tell you that explosive emotions are not logical. They might say, "Anger won't bring them back," or "He didn't mean to die, so don't be mad at him." Watch out. You might find yourself buying into this rational thinking. That's just the problem—***thinking is logical; feeling is not.***

Remind yourself that explosive emotions do not have to be logical. They are not good or bad, right or wrong. Don't judge your feelings; experience them. Your feelings are your own, and they need to be acknowledged and expressed.

Our society is often quick to stifle, repress, or deny you the right to have explosive emotions, particularly when you have experienced a loss. Demonstrating emotional hurts is judged as wrong. You may have discovered an unspoken expectation that you are responsible for "keeping it together." Be forewarned—what you do with these emotions can have a powerful impact on your grief experience. If you collaborate with the well-intentioned but misinformed people around you, your body, mind, and spirit will probably be damaged in the process.

If explosive emotions are part of your journey, be aware that you have two avenues for expression—outward or inward. The outward avenue leads to healing; the inward avenue does not. Critical to your healing is finding someone who doesn't judge you but allows you to feel whatever you do.

Explosive emotions may surface at any time when someone you have loved dies. You cry out in anguish, "How could this happen?", "This isn't fair!", "My life has been turned upside down." You may direct these emotions toward the person who died, friends and family members, doctors, God, people who have not experienced loss, or toward life in general. Your personal experience with explosive emotions will be unique. The key to understanding this dimension of the grief journey: ***explosive emotions must be expressed, not repressed!***

The anger you may feel toward your God or a Higher Power deserves special mention here. In my counseling with bereaved people, they have taught me that they get angry at themselves for being angry at God. At times, this admonishment is further reinforced by people around who say, "Don't be angry at God!" Actually, being angry at God speaks of having a relationship with God in the first place. If you feel anger at your God, express it!

One last thought about explosive emotions. Be careful. Do not direct your explosive emotions inwardly. If you do so, rather than "talking out" your feelings, you may suffer chronic feelings of low self-esteem, depression, feelings of guilt, physical complaints, and perhaps even persistent thoughts of suicide. If you have already experienced these feelings, get help immediately. You have a wound that needs attention right now.

Experiencing explosive emotions is normal. They should, however, change in intensity and duration as you do the work of mourning. Again, I want to emphasize that the key is finding someone who will help you understand what you are feeling and allow you to embrace your grief. Remember—you can't go around your grief, or over it, or under it—you must go through it. Hopefully, on your grief journey you will be surrounded by people who understand, support, and love you and who will help you explore your explosive emotions without trying to stifle you.

Self Inventory

In the space provided, complete the following thought: "My experience with explosive emotions is or has been . . . "

Self-care Guidelines

Ultimately, helping yourself heal requires that explosive emotions be expressed, not repressed, or worse yet, totally denied. Don't prescribe these emotions for yourself but be alert for them. You will need a supportive listener who can tolerate, encourage, and validate your explosive emotions without judging, retaliating, or arguing with you. The comforting presence of someone who cares will help you seek continued self-understanding of your grief experience.

Be aware, though, of the difference between the right to feel explosive emotions and the right to act out these feelings and actions. It's all right to feel angry. But if you hurt others, yourself, or destroy property, the people who care about you will need to set limits on your behavior. This distinction is important to remember as you allow yourself to mourn. Also, remind yourself that explosive emotions can often indicate underlying feelings of pain, helplessness, frustrations, fear, and hurt. Listen to your explosive emotions, and you may discover the need to embrace these feelings.

Keep telling yourself that explosive emotions are not good or bad, right or wrong. They are your feelings and a symptom of an injury that needs nurturing, not judging. Paradoxically, the way to diminish explosive emotions is to experience them. Although, at times, you may express anger and other explosive emotions in irrational ways, friends, family, and helpers who fail to allow you to express yourself leave you feeling abandoned, guilty, and confused.

You might want to review what you just noted under your **Self Inventory.** Then, find a friend or understanding counselor who will explore these experiences with you. Your stabilizing helper can listen and "walk with you" as you express whatever you need to talk out.

Personal Self-care Inventory

In the space provided on the next page, write out what you are doing, or have done to help yourself with explosive emotions:

GUILT AND REGRET

As part of your grief journey, you may experience feelings of guilt and self-blame. You possibly have even said or thought things like "If only I could have gotten him to the doctor sooner . . . " or "If only I had insisted that she take better care of herself," or "If only I wouldn't have let him drive the car that day."

If you find yourself having some of these "If only's . . ." be compassionate with yourself. When someone you care about dies, it's natural to think about actions you could or could not have taken to prevent the death. You simply are unable to go through life in close relationships with other people without saying or doing something you later wish you could change.

While these feelings of guilt or regret are natural, they are sometimes not logical to those people around you. They may say things like, "Don't even think about it; there was nothing you could have done." Warning! Don't allow others to explain away what you are thinking and feeling. Doing so is not helpful.

Other aspects of guilt and regret also are worth review. Note if any of the following are, or have been, a part of your grief experience.

Survival Guilt

Sometimes being alive when someone you love has died can cause survival guilt. Have you found yourself thinking, "How could he or she have died, and I survived?" This is a natural question. It is a part of your grief experience. Find someone who will be understanding and allow you to talk it out.

Relief-guilt Syndrome

Relief-guilt syndrome is when you feel guilty for being relieved when someone loved dies. This syndrome often occurs when the person who died had been ill for a long time. You may not miss frequent trips to the hospital or the demanding physical responsibilities of caring for that person.

Relief-guilt also occurs when you recognize you will not miss certain aspects of the relationship. For example, you may not miss how he never cleaned up after himself. Or you won't miss her annoying habit of never closing cabinet doors. Or you won't miss being slightly late for church because he was always running behind schedule.

To miss some things about the person who has died is all right and perfectly natural. If, however, you acknowledge this sense of relief as a demonstration of lack of love, you may continue to feel guilty for being relieved. An understanding listener can help you explore this as a part of your work of mourning.

Long-standing Personality Factors

Some individuals have felt guilty their entire lives. Hopefully, you are not one of them, but it is possible. Why? Some people learn early in life, typically during childhood, that they are responsible when anything bad occurs. When someone dies, it is just one more thing about which to feel guilty. If all-encompassing guilt is part of your experience, find a professional counseling relationship that can help you work on understanding the nature and extent of your feelings.

Joy-guilt Syndrome

Reexperiencing any kind of joy in life after someone loved dies can also make you feel guilty. As you do the work of mourning, a day will come where you experience a laugh, a smile, a happy feeling. Great! Why should you feel depressed forever? This syndrome usually relates to your loyalty to the person who died. You may fear that being happy in some way betrays the relationship you once had. Talking about these feelings with a caring listener will help you heal.

Magical Thinking and Guilt

Consciously (or unconsciously) wishing for the death of someone loved also may cause you to experience feelings of guilt. It is, however, an example of "magical thinking" that somehow your thoughts could cause that action.

At some point in your relationship, you may have thought, "I wish you would go away and leave me alone." Or, if the relationship was very difficult, you may even have had more direct thoughts of actually wanting the relationship to end. If so, you may now feel somehow responsible for the death.

All relationships have periods when negative thoughts occur. Obviously, however, your mind doesn't have the power to inflict death. If you are struggling with any of these thoughts, find someone to talk with who will be understanding and non-judgmental.

Do not allow feelings of guilt or regret to go unexpressed. They are a natural part of your journey. Yet, while they are normal, these feelings still need to be explored. So don't try to make this journey alone. Find a compassionate partner!

Self Inventory

In the space provided on the next page, complete the following thought: "My experience with guilt and regret is or has been . . ."

Self-care Guidelines

If any aspect of guilt and regret are a part of your grief experience, look for a compassionate, patient, and non-judgmental listener. If you feel it, acknowledge it, and express these feelings openly.

Do not allow people to explain your feelings away. While they are trying to help, this attitude will not allow you to "talk out" what you think and feel on the inside. When you explore these feelings of guilt and regret, you will come to understand the limits of your own responsibility.

As you express yourself, remember—you are not perfect; no one is. Something happened that you wish had not. Someone you care about has died. Now, you will naturally go back and review if you could have said or done anything to change this difficult reality. Allow yourself this review time, but as you do so, be compassionate with yourself. Continue to remind yourself some things in life you can not change.

One of the worst things you could do is to ignore or repress feelings of guilt. Many physical and emotional problems will result when you try to push these feelings away without talking them out. If feelings of guilt or regret are complicating your healing, don't be ashamed to find a trained professional helper.

Personal Self-care Inventory

In the space provided, write out what you are doing, or
have done, to help yourself with any feelings of guilt and
regret:

LOSS, EMPTINESS,
SADNESS, DEPRESSION

With good reason, loss, emptiness, sadness, and depression
can be a dimension of your grief journey. Someone you love
has died, and you hurt. Unfortunately, our culture has an
unwritten rule that says while physical illness can't be helped,
you are responsible for your emotional well-being. In other
words, some people think you should be able to "control"
your feelings of loss, emptiness, sadness, and depression.

Nothing could be further from the truth. Your sadness
is a symptom of your wound. Just as physical wounds require
attention, so do emotional wounds. Paradoxically, the only
way to lessen your pain is to move toward it, not away from
it.

Moving toward your sadness is not easy to do. Every
time you admit feeling sad, people around you may say things
like, "Don't be sad," "Get a hold of yourself," or "Well, just
think about what you have to be thankful for." Comments

like these hinder, not help, your healing. If your heart and soul are prevented from feeling the sadness, odds are your body may be harmed in the process. You have been emotionally, physically, and spiritually injured. Now you must listen to your sadness.

Your full sense of loss will never occur all at once. Each passing day, you will not necessarily feel any better. Yet, time will help you heal if you learn to embrace your hurt. By doing so, you empower yourself to heal. As you are willing to move toward your sadness, you will discover continued meaning and purpose in life.

Weeks, or often months, pass before you are fully confronted by the depth of your sadness. This slowly growing awareness is good. You could not or should not tolerate all of your sadness at once. Your body, mind, and spirit need time working together to allow you to embrace the depth of your loss, emptiness, and sadness. Be patient with yourself. Surround yourself with loving people who will understand, not judge, you. Keep in mind, a vital part of your life is no longer present. You have every right to feel loss, emptiness, and sadness. I suggest you say it out loud right now—"I HAVE EVERY RIGHT TO FEEL LOSS, EMPTINESS, AND SADNESS!"

Take a moment to write in the space provided what times of the day, week, month, or year bring about feelings of heightened loss, emptiness, and sadness:

Now that you have written your own naturally difficult times, let me share with you some common ones gathered from personal experience and the experience of other bereaved people. Difficult times include weekends, holidays, bedtimes, waking in the morning, awakening late at night, family meals, arriving home to an empty house, and any kind of anniversary occasions. These difficult times usually have a special connection to the person who has died.

Occasionally, your feelings of loss, emptiness, and sadness can be overwhelming enough to be classified as a "clinical depression." After all, grief and mourning go hand in hand with many symptoms of depression such as sleep disturbance, appetite disturbance, decreased energy, withdrawal, guilt, dependency, lack of concentration, and a sense of losing control.

Any changes in your usual ability to perform at work or home can result in feelings of. isolation and helplessness. If you feel totally immobilized, please get help from understanding friends or a professional counselor. Do not try to face your depression alone.

Depression, however, can often be difficult to detect. Symptoms may be present, but they go unobserved. This situation is referred to as "masked depression." A few examples of masked, or unrecognized depression, may include sleeping too much, uncontrollable hostility, overeating, alcohol and/or drug abuse, and multiple physical complaints where nothing can be found to treat. If these are a part of your experience, please find someone to help you heal yourself.

Thoughts of suicide also may occur during your grief journey. Hundreds of bereaved people have shared with me thoughts like, "I'm not sure I'd mind if I didn't wake up tomorrow." Comments like this reflect a need to further explore the depth of your loss, emptiness, and sadness. It's natural to experience these suicidal thoughts; it is not natural to want to take your own life when someone in your life dies.

If you have been thinking of taking your own life, talk to a professional helper trained to help you. Suicidal thoughts are sometimes an expression of wanting to find relief from the pain of your grief. Yes, you have been injured and you hurt. But to help your injury heal, you must openly talk out what this death has meant to you.

Self Inventory

In the space provided, complete the following thought: "My experience with loss, emptiness, and sadness is or has been . . . "

Self-care Guidelines

As you embrace your feelings of loss, emptiness, and sadness, you will need the comfort of trusted people—close friends or compassionate professional helpers. The feelings described above can leave you feeling isolated and alone; consequently, you will need to talk them out with accepting and understanding people. Talk to them about the death and its meaning to you.

Keep talking until you have exhausted your capacity to talk. Doing so will help reconnect you with the world outside of yourself. Or if you can't talk it out, write it out! But get the feelings outside of yourself. And beyond talking and writing, give yourself permission to cry. That means crying as much and as often as you need to. Tears can help cleanse your body, mind, and spirit!

As you embrace your sadness, you need people to validate what you feel. A good analogy is that you need someone to walk with you, not in front of or behind you. When you acknowledge these feelings in the presence of a trusted friend or professional helper, you are allowing yourself to heal. As you hurt, you heal.

Most importantly, remember temporary feelings of depression have value in your grief journey. Being depressed doesn't mean you are incompetent. Or it doesn't mean you should feel abandoned. Actually, depression is nature's way of allowing for a time-out while you heal the wounds of your grief. Depression slows down your body and prevents major organ systems from being damaged. Depression allows you to turn inward and slow down your spirit, too. It aids in your healing and provides time to slowly begin re-ordering your life. These natural feelings associated with grief can ultimately help you move ahead, to assess old ways of being, and to make plans for the future.

Personal Self-care Inventory

In the space provided, write out what you are doing, or have done, to help yourself with loss, emptiness, sadness, and depression:

RELIEF, RELEASE

A dimension of your grief experience may be the feelings of relief or release when someone you love dies. This feeling is normal and natural. The death may bring relief from suffering, particularly when the illness has been long and debilitating. Your feeling of relief does not, however, equate to a lack of love for the person in your life who died.

The feelings of relief and release also relate to the reality that you do not begin grieving at the moment of someone's death. The experience of grief and the need to mourn actually begin when the person you love enters the transition from living to dying. Your grief starts when you are watching someone you love endure physical pain and loss of quality of life. Doing so is draining emotionally, physically, and spiritually. In certain circumstances when the person you love dies, you have every right to feel a sense of relief—for them and for you.

Another form of relief you may experience comes when you finally express your thoughts and feelings about the death. If you have repressed or denied these feelings before, you may feel as if some pressure has been released from your head, heart, and soul.

Being able to acknowledge relief as a part of your grief experience can be a critical step in your healing. Working to embrace these feelings creates the opportunity to find hope in your healing.

Self Inventory

In the space provided below and on the next page, complete the following thought: "My experience with relief and release is or has been . . ."

Self-care Guidelines

If you feel a sense of relief or release, write about it, or better yet, talk it out. Again, find someone you trust who will listen and hear you. If you feel guilty about being relieved, talk about it with someone who can help you feel understood. Whatever you do, don't isolate yourself. Talk about your feelings!

Personal Self-care Inventory

In the space provided, write out what you are doing, or have done, to help yourself with any feelings of relief and release:

CHAPTER **V**

AM I CRAZY?

"Grief is like a long, winding valley where any bend may reveal a totally new landscape"

C.S. Lewis

Other aspects of grief and mourning are explored in this chapter. They may or may not be a part of your personal experience. As mentioned previously, my intent is not to prescribe what should be happening to you. Instead, I encourage you to become familiar with what you may encounter while you grieve and do your work of mourning.

TIME DISTORTION

"I don't know what day it is, let alone what time it is!" This kind of comment is not unusual when you are mourning. Sometimes, time moves so quickly; at other times, it merely crawls. Your sense of past and future also may seem to be frozen in place. You may lose track of what day or even what month it is.

This normal experience of time distortion often plays a part in the "going crazy syndrome" described in Chapter IV. No, you are not crazy. But if you don't know this is normal, you may think you are.

In the space provided, complete the following thought: "My experience with time distortion has been to date . . ."

OBSESSIVE REVIEW OR RUMINATING

Obsessive review or ruminating are the psychological terms used for describing how you may repeat the circumstances about the death or stories about the person who has died. It's "telling your story" over and over again. In your grief journey, you may often review events of the death and memories of the person who died over and over. This normal process helps bring your head and your heart together! Allow yourself to do this. Blocking it out won't help you heal. Don't be angry with yourself if you can't seem to stop wanting to repeat your story. Review or rumination is a powerful and necessary part of the hard work of mourning.

Yes, it hurts to constantly think and talk about the person you loved so much. But, remember—all grief wounds get worse before they get better. Be compassionate with yourself. Try to surround yourself with people who allow and encourage you to repeat whatever you need to tell again.

In the space provided on the next page, complete the following thought: "My experience with telling my experience over and over again is or has been . . ."

SEARCH FOR MEANING

Naturally, you try to make sense of why someone you love died. You may find yourself asking questions like "Why him or her?" "Why now?" or "Why this way?" Yes, you have questions. You are human and are simply trying to understand your experience. No, answers won't always be, and often aren't, specific to your questions. Yet, you still need to give yourself permission to ask them.

As you wrestle with "why?" you may be outraged at your God or Higher Power. You may feel a stagnation or disillusionment with your spiritual life as you embrace your pain. On the other hand, you feel closer than ever before. You can only be where you are.

You may be able to come up with dozens of reasons why the person who died should not have died under these circumstances or at this time. Whatever the nature or number of your questions, asking them is a normal part of your grief journey.

As you explore the meaning of this experience through your questions, be certain not to commit "spiritual suicide." Do not prohibit yourself from asking the questions you know are within you. If you do, you may shut down your capacity to give and receive love during this vulnerable period in your life.

Be aware that people may try to tell you not to ask questions about your personal search for meaning in your grief journey. Or worse yet, watch out for people who always try to have easy answers to your difficult questions. Most bereaved people do not find comfort in pat responses; neither will you. The healing occurs in posing the questions in the first place, not just in finding answers.

Find a friend, group, or counselor who will understand your need to search for meaning and be supportive without attempting to offer answers. Companionship and responsive listening can help you explore your religious and spiritual values, question your philosophy of life, and renew your resources for living!

In the space provided, complete the following thought: "My experience with a search for meaning is or has been. . ."

IS THIS DEATH GOD'S WILL?

Closely related to the search for meaning is the commonly asked question, "Is this death God's will?" If you have a perception of an all-powerful God or Higher Power, you probably find this question particularly difficult.

Sometimes you may reason: "God loves me, so why take this most precious person from me?" Or you may have been told, "It is God's will, and you should just accept it and go on." If you, however, internalize this message, you may repress your grief and ignore your human need to mourn.

Repressing your grief because you need to "just accept it and go on" can be self-destructive. If you don't ask questions and if you don't express feelings, you may ultimately drown in despair. If your soul does not ask, your body will probably protest. Repressing and denying heart-felt questions can, and often does, keep your wounds from healing. Listen to your questions!

In the space provided, complete the following thought: "My experience with questioning 'Is this God's will' is or has been. . ."

TRANSITIONAL OBJECTS

Transitional objects are belongings of the person in your life who died. They often can give you comfort. Objects such as clothing, books, or prized possessions can help you feel close to someone you miss so much.

For example, during my counseling with a bereaved woman, she shared with me that she found it comforting to take one of her husband's favorite shirts to bed with her. She said, "As I clutched his shirt close to me, I didn't feel so alone. But as I worked with my grief, my need for the shirt dwindled over time."

Some people may try to distance you from belongings such as the shirt described above. This behavior fits with the tendency in our culture to move away from grief instead of toward it.

Remember—embrace the comfort provided by familiar objects. To do away with them too soon takes away a sense of security these belongings provide. Once you have moved toward reconciliation, you will probably be better able to decide what to do with them. Some things, however, you may want to keep forever. That's all right, too. Simply giving away the belongings of the person you loved does not equate with healing in your grief.

Nor does keeping some belongings mean you have "created a shrine." This phrase is used when someone keeps everything just as it was for years after the death. Creating a shrine, however, only prevents acknowledging the painful new reality that someone you love has died. Understanding the difference between transitional objects and creating a shrine is important. The former helps you heal; the latter does not.

In the space provided, complete the following thought: "My experience with transitional objects is, or has been . . ."

SUICIDAL THOUGHTS

While we explored suicidal thoughts in the last chapter, it is important enough to reemphasize here. Thoughts that come and go about questioning if you want to go on living can be a normal part of your grief and mourning. You might say or think, "I'm not sure I'd mind it if I didn't wake up in the morning." Often this thought is not so much an active wish to kill yourself as it is a wish to ease your pain.

To have these thoughts is normal; however, to make plans and take action to end your life is abnormal. Sometimes your body, mind, and spirit can hurt so much you wonder if you will ever feel alive again. Just remember that in accomplishing the hard work of mourning, you can and will find continued meaning in your life. Let yourself be helped as you have hope for your healing.

If thoughts of suicide take on planning and structure, make certain that you get help immediately. Sometimes tunnel vision can prevent you from seeing choices. Please choose to go on living as you honor the memory of the person in your life who has died.

In the space provided, complete the following thought: "My experience with suicidal thoughts or not wanting to go on living is or has been . . ."

GRIEF ATTACKS OR MEMORY EMBRACES

"I was just sailing along feeling pretty good, when out of nowhere came this overwhelming feeling of grief." This comment often reflects what is commonly called a *"grief attack."* Another term I use for this experience is a *"memory embrace."* A grief attack or memory embrace is a period of time when you may have intense anxiety and sharp pain.

You may think that long periods of deep depression are the most common part of grief and mourning. Actually, you may more frequently encounter acute and episodic "pangs" or "spasms" of grief. That's why they are called grief attacks. They sometimes "attack" you out of nowhere.

You may feel an overwhelming sense of missing the person you loved and find yourself openly crying, or perhaps even sobbing. As one woman reflected, "I'll be busy for awhile, and sometimes even forget he has died. Then I'll see his picture or think of his favorite food, and I'll just feel like I can't even move."

Grief attacks are normal. When and if one strikes you, be compassionate with yourself. You have every right to miss the person who has died and to feel temporary paralysis. Whatever you do, don't try to deny a grief attack when you experience it. It is probably more powerful than you are.

I like to think of grief attacks as a reflection of how those we love are determined not to be forgotten. Although the pain of a grief attack hurts so deeply, embrace it, or you can risk emotional, spiritual, and physical paralysis.

In the space provided below and on the next page, complete the following thought: "My experience with grief attacks or memory embraces is or has been. . ."

ANNIVERSARY AND HOLIDAY
GRIEF OCCASIONS

Naturally, anniversary and holiday occasions can bring about "pangs" of grief. Birthdays; wedding dates; holidays such as Easter, Thanksgiving, Hanukkah, Christmas; and other special occasions create a heightened sense of loss. At these times, you may likely experience a grief attack or memory embrace.

Your "pangs" of grief also may occur in response to circumstances that bring about reminders of the painful absence of someone in your life. For many families, certain times have special meaning related to family togetherness, and the person who died is more deeply missed at those times. For example, the beginning of Spring, the first snowfall, an annual Fourth of July party, or anytime when activities were shared as a couple or a family.

Perhaps the most important thing to remember is that these reactions are natural. Sometimes the anticipation of an anniversary or holiday actually turns out to be worse than the day itself.

Interestingly enough, sometimes your internal clock will alert you to an anniversary date you may have forgotten. If you notice you are feeling down or experiencing "pangs" of grief, you may be having an anniversary response. Keep in mind that it is normal.

Plan ahead when you know some naturally painful times are coming for you. Unfortunately, some bereaved people will not mention anniversaries, holidays, or special occasions to anyone. As a result, they suffer in silence, and their feelings of isolation increase. Don't let this happen to you. Recognize you will need support and map out how to get it! You will find some helpful guidelines for surviving your grief attacks during anniversaries and special occasions in Chapter VIII.

In the space provided, complete the following thought: "My experience with anniversary and holiday grief occasions (include other special occasions that apply to you) is or has been . . ."

SUDDEN CHANGES IN MOOD

When someone loved dies, you may feel like you are surviving fairly well one minute and in the depths of despair the next. Sudden changes in your mood are a difficult, yet natural, part of your grief journey. These mood changes can be small or very dramatic. They can be triggered by driving past a familiar place, a song, an insensitive comment, or even changes in the weather.

Mood changes cause confusion because your inappropriate self-expectation may be that you should follow a pattern of continually feeling better. You probably also have some people around you who share this expectation. Attack this inappropriate expectation and be self-nurturing as you embrace the ebbs and flows of mood changes.

If you have these ups and downs, don't be hard on yourself. Be patient with yourself. As you do the work of mourning and move toward healing, the periods of hopelessness will be replaced by periods of hopefulness. During these times, you also can benefit from a support system that understands these mood changes as normal.

In the space provided, complete the following thought: "My experience with sudden changes in mood is or has been . . ."

IDENTIFICATION SYMPTOMS OF PHYSICAL ILLNESS

When you care deeply about someone and they die, you sometimes develop ways to identify with and feel close to that person. One way is by relating to the physical symptoms of the person who died. For example, if she died from a brain tumor you may have more frequent headaches. If he died from a heart attack, you may have chest pains. Of course, to check for organic problems is important, but you also should be aware that you might be experiencing identification symptoms of physical illness. Bereaved people have shared with me these examples:

"She had awful pain in her stomach, and after she died I began to have them, too. It kind of made me feel close to her. After awhile the stomach pain went away and I felt some sense of loss. As I have healed, I've been able to let go of the stomach pain."

"I loved him so much. After he died, I wanted to be just like him. One of the ways I did it was to be dizzy just like he used to be all the time."

Don't be shocked if you have a few physical symptoms like the person who died. Your body is responding to the loss. As you do the hard work of mourning, however, these symptoms should go away. If not, find someone who will listen to you and help you understand what is happening. Also, not everyone will experience these symptoms, and you may be one of those people.

In the space provided, complete the following thought: "My experience with identification symptoms is, or has been . . ."

POWERLESSNESS AND HELPLESSNESS

Although often ignored, your grief can at times leave you feeling powerless. You may think or say, "What am I going to do? I feel so completely helpless." While part of you realizes you had no control over what happened, another part feels a sense of powerlessness at not having been able to prevent it. You would like to have your life back to the way it was, but you can't. You may think, hope, wish, and pray the death could be reversed, but feel powerless to do anything about it.

Also, you may wonder if somehow you would have acted differently or been more assertive, you could have prevented the death. Your "if only's" and "what if's" are often expressions of wishing you could have been more powerful or control something you could not. Lack of control is a difficult reality to accept. Yet, it is a reality that over time and through the work of mourning you must encounter. These feelings of helplessness and powerlessness in the face of this painful reality are normal and natural.

Almost paradoxically, by acknowledging and allowing for temporary feelings of helplessness, you ultimately become helpful to yourself. When you try to "stay strong" you often get yourself into trouble. Share your feelings with caring people around you. Remember—shared grief is diminished grief; find someone to talk to who will listen without judging.

In the space provided, complete the following thought: "My experience with powerlessness and helplessness is or has been . . ."

CRYING AND SOBBING

Yes, your tears may flow. Your heart, head, and spirit may sob. Why? Tears are the body's means of relieving internal tension, and they allow you to communicate a need to be comforted. I once heard someone say "crying is what you do when you can't do anything else."

Tears and sobbing are much healthier responses to a loss than repressing and denying your emotions. Some people around you, however, may associate tears of grief with personal inadequacy and weakness. This association isn't unusual in a culture that makes you feel ashamed to openly express feelings of loss and grief.

Don't be surprised if your tears generate feelings of helplessness in your friends, family, and caregivers. Out of a desire to protect you from pain (and often their own pain) people may say, "Tears won't bring him back" and "He wouldn't want you to cry." Internalizing these messages is harmful and may inhibit the natural expression of your tears.

Ever notice how our society has an interesting perception of who does well "handling grief" and who doesn't do well? Often, the stoic, emotionless person who seems to "have it together" is perceived as doing well. The one who openly cries or sobs is often labeled "out of control" or as someone who has "lost it." Actually, nothing could be further from the truth.

Early in your grief, you may not be able to cry. That's all right, too. The lack of tears at that point in the grief journey may signal feelings of shock and numbness. In my experience, tears have a way of coming when they are ready. However, if you feel a need to cry and you can't, you may benefit by seeing a skilled counselor. He or she will be able to recognize when tears are struggling to emerge. The counselor also will recognize the uniqueness of your need and ability to cry.

For example, perhaps you have not cried in fifty years. As a result you may not even remember what crying feels like. Or, if you are a man, maybe you have been conditioned throughout your life not to cry. If you are a woman, on the other hand, tears may come more easily. A skilled counselor will recognize and respect these differences.

While crying at first may be difficult, as the reality of the death begins to sink in, you may not just cry, but sob. Sobbing is like wailing, and it comes from the inner core of your being. Sobbing is an expression of the deep, strong emotions within you. These emotions need to get out, and sobbing allows for the release of your physical, emotional, and spiritual energy.

In many Eastern cultures, sobbing and deep wailing are encouraged and understood as a normal part of grief and mourning. In our culture, however, sobbing is often considered frightening. It is perceived as being "out of control." But as you sob, in reality you are confronting the depth of your pain and feeling of loss.

Crying or sobbing—do what you need to do with your tears—don't try to be strong and brave for yourself or others. Tears have a voice of their own. You will be wise to allow yours to speak to you. Listen to your tears and heal.

In the space provided, complete the following thought: "My experience with crying and sobbing is or has been . . ."

DREAMS

Dreaming about the person in your life who has died may be a part of your grief journey. If it is, remember no one is a better expert than you are in understanding what your dreams mean to you.

Dreams are one of the ways the work of mourning takes place. They may or may not play an important part in your experience. A dream, for example, may reflect a searching for the person who has died. Dreams also provide opportunities—to feel close to someone loved who died, to embrace the reality of the death, to gently confront the depth of the loss, to renew memories, or to develop a new self-identity. Dreams also may help you search for meaning in life and death or explore unfinished business. Finally, dreams can show you hope for the future. The content of your dreams often reflects changes in your experience with mourning. So if dreams are part of your journey, make use of them to better understand where you have been, where you are, and where you are going. Also, find a skilled listener who won't interpret your dreams for you, but who will listen with you!

On the other hand, you may experience nightmares, particularly after traumatic, violent deaths. These dreams can be very frightening. If your dreams are distressing, talk about them to someone who can support and understand you.

In the space provided, complete the following thought: "My experience with dreams or nightmares is or has been . . ."

MYSTICAL EXPERIENCES

When someone loved dies, you may possibly have experiences that are not always rationally explainable. However, that doesn't mean something is wrong with these experiences. The sad reality is if you share these experiences with others, you may be considered "mentally ill." In fact, you are actually mystically sensitive.

The primary form of mystical experience that bereaved people have taught me about is communicating with the person who died. Some people find the experience hard to believe and try to explain it away in a rational manner: "I must have been dreaming," or "I was probably half-asleep." Others try to distance themselves from the experience because they are taught that such things are impossible: "A rational mind just doesn't experience those kinds of things." So, if you want to be considered "rational" or "sane," what would make sense is for you to feel compelled to distance yourself from this kind of "irrational" experience.

Types of mystical experiences vary. In Alabama, for example, a mother, whose daughter had died, woke up one summer morning. She looked out the window and saw it snowing in her yard only. The snow lasted for 15 minutes and then stopped. The mother understood this as a communication telling her that her daughter was all right and not to worry so much. In another instance, a man, whose wife had died, saw her laying on the couch in his living room. "It's like she came to me and wrapped me in her arms. I felt warm and happy . . . I experienced her presence."

I have listened and learned from hundreds of people who have experienced seeing, hearing, and feeling the presence of someone who has died. I am a scientist and supposed to be "rational." I can only tell you to remain open to experiences in this realm. Don't judge yourself or others who have these mystical experiences. Or if you don't have any mystical experiences, don't think that something is wrong with you.

In the space provided on the next page, complete the following thought: "My experience with mystical experiences is or has been . . ."

LOSS OF INTIMACY
AND SEXUALITY

Often bereaved people ignore this area of loss following the death of someone loved. Yet, a basic human need is to feel close to others and to give and receive love. If your life partner has died, your loss also includes kissing, hugging, and physically touching someone to whom you felt close for so long.

In some cases, the person who died may have been ill for quite a while. So physical intimacy in terms of intercourse may have been missing as well. Keep in mind, however, intercourse is only one way of expressing intimacy and love for someone. It is certainly not the only way.

Loss of intimacy can occur not only in couple relationships but also in other relationships. To no longer hug your small child, to no longer embrace an adult son or daughter, or to no longer touch or be touched by someone you love— all can strike the depths of your feelings of loss.

Don't deny or minimize this part of your grief experience. Use the space provided to write about it or talk it out. Ignoring this loss will only make it more difficult.

In the space provided, complete the following thought: "My experience with loss of intimacy or sexuality is, or has been. . ."

DRUGS, ALCOHOL, AND GRIEF

Unfortunately, when someone loved dies, you may be tempted to quickly erase your feelings of grief. This desire to avoid and to mask the pain is understandable. To do so, however, only brings temporary relief from a hurt that must ultimately be embraced.

To mourn means to express your thoughts and feelings outside of yourself. If you are inappropriately given tranquilizers or other prescriptive drugs to "give you relief," "calm you down," or "numb you out," you may not have the opportunity to express yourself.

Despite beliefs that you can chemically push feelings away, prescribing medication during times of acute grief is usually motivated by a need to protect you from your feelings. Yes, you hurt. You have every right to hurt. But to automatically give you a psychoactive medication intended to change your emotional and physical state communicates what you are feeling is wrong or bad. This notion goes back to how our society often shames you for outwardly expressing your grief.

My comments are not intended to suggest that the use of medication with someone who is bereaved is never appropriate. For example, you may become both physically and emotionally exhausted after going a prolonged time without sleep. Obviously, energy is used in doing the work of mourning. Careful assessment may indicate the need for limited night-time sedation if you have prolonged insomnia.

In addition, other situations may be indications for medications as being appropriate. However, be informed about why you need a medication, what it is intended for, and any side effects you might anticipate. Monitor how you use the drug so it doesn't result in an inappropriate dependency. If you are too overwhelmed to monitor any medication, involve someone else who can be an informed assistant to you.

I would be remiss if I didn't mention that alcohol abuse and dependence are something for which to watch. Not by chance alone has alcohol use and abuse become a problem for many people. Experience suggests that alcohol is perhaps the most common form of self-medication for the bereaved.

Many subcultures in our society condone and encourage the use of alcohol during times of bereavement. Because alcohol can become psychologically as well as physically addicting, however, a pattern of continued use and abuse can occur. Some people become dependent on alcohol, and, as a result, an entirely new set of problems come about. As the amount of alcohol consumed increases, so do difficulties with feeling agitated and depressed. In addition, sleeping and eating problems can occur.

If you suspect you might have an alcohol or drug problem, you will be wise to seek help from a trained drug and alcohol counselor. Healing comes through expression of thoughts and feelings, not through becoming abusive or dependent on drugs of any kind.

In the space provided on the next page, complete the following thought: "My experience with drugs and alcohol is or has been . . ."

SELF-FOCUS

The very nature of your grief requires a self-focus or a turning inward. This temporary self-focus is necessary for your long-term survival. Turning inward helps you feel protected from an outside world that may be frightening right now.

Some people may try to "take your grief away from you" by preventing you from any kind of self-focus. They may want you to quickly re-enter the outside world without understanding your need for a temporary retreat. If turning inward is part of your experience, be assured you are normal.

The word TEMPORARY, in relationship to this self-focus, is important. You may move back and forth between needing time alone and time with other people. Be aware, however, if you stay only in a self-focused, inward mode, you may risk development of a pattern of not sharing your grief. As you well know by now, not sharing your grief will stunt your healing process.

When you are in pain following the death of someone loved, the turning inward and the need for self-focus is analogous to what occurs when you have a physical wound. You cover a physical wound with a bandage for a period of time. Then you expose the wound to the open air which contains healing properties as well as contaminants. The emotional, physical, and spiritual pain of grief certainly demands the same kind of respect.

In the space provided, complete the following thought: "My experience with self-focus is or has been. . ."

CHAPTER

RECONCILIATION
AS HEALING

The process of healing in your grief calls on all of your personal resources. As you know by now, grief and mourning are powerful experiences. So is your ability to help yourself heal. In doing the work of mourning, you are moving toward your healing. Some people may tell you to "resolve" or "get over" your grief. Don't believe them. As a human being, you don't "get over" grief. You live with it and work to "reconcile" yourself to it.

A number of psychological models describing grief refer to "resolution," "recovery," "reestablishment," or "reorganization" as being the final dimension of your experience. These words suggest a total return to your normal life or the life you experienced before the death. Yet in my experience, everyone is changed forever by the grief journey.

Yes, you are changed. The death of someone loved alters your life forever. The issue is not that you will never be happy again. It is simply that you will never be exactly the same as you were before the death. Some people want desperately for you to just "get with it" and be just like you were before. To assume this is possible is unrealistic and often damaging.

Healing in grief is not a perfect state, reestablishment, or recovery. You can and probably will have pangs of grief years after the death. That recurrence of painful feelings doesn't mean anything is wrong with you. Healing does not mean forgetting.

In exploring what your ultimate healing goal will be, I ask you to consider using the term *"reconciliation."* I believe this term is more expressive of what occurs as you work to integrate the new reality of moving forward in life without the physical presence of the person who has died.

If you do the hard work of mourning, you can and will experience reconciliation: a renewed sense of energy and confidence, an ability to acknowledge the full reality of the death, and the capacity to become re-involved with the activities of living. Remember—healing is a process, not an event. Reconciling your grief takes longer and involves more labor than most people are aware.

Embrace your grief and share it outside yourself. When you do, it will change from being ever-present, sharp, and stinging to a renewed sense of meaning and purpose. Your sense of loss does not just disappear; it softens, and the intense pangs of grief become less frequent.

To help you explore where you are in your movement toward reconciliation, the following criteria that suggest healing may be helpful. You don't have to meet each of these criteria for healing to be taking place. Again, remember that reconciliation is an ongoing process. If you are early on in the work of your mourning, you may not meet any of these criteria. But this list will give you a way to monitor your movement toward healing. You may want to place check marks beside those criteria you believe you meet.

CRITERIA FOR RECONCILIATION

As you embrace your grief and do the work of mourning, you can and will be able to demonstrate the majority of the following:

- A recognition of the reality and finality of the death of the person who has died.

- A return to stable eating and sleeping patterns that were present prior to the death.

- A renewed sense of release or relief from the person who has died. You will have thoughts about the person, but you will not be preoccupied with these thoughts.

- The capacity to enjoy experiences in life that are normally enjoyable.

- The establishment of new and healthy relationships.

- The capacity to live a full life without feelings of guilt or lack of self-respect.

- The capacity to organize and plan one's life toward the future.

- The capacity to become comfortable with the way things are rather than attempting to make things as they were.

- The capacity to welcome more change in your life.

- The awareness that you have allowed yourself to fully grieve, and you have survived.

- The awareness that you do not "get over your grief;" instead, you have a new reality, meaning, and purpose in your life.

- The capacity to acknowledge new parts of yourself that you have discovered in your grief journey.

- The capacity to adjust to the new role changes that have resulted from the loss of the relationship.

- The capacity to be compassionate with yourself when normal resurgences of intense grief occur (holiday, anniversaries, special occasions).

- The capacity to acknowledge that the pain of loss is an inherent part of life resulting from the ability to give and receive love.

Self Inventory

In the space provided, take the opportunity to write where you think you are in your own unique healing process. As you have learned about the concept of "reconciliation," what thoughts come to mind? Be compassionate with yourself if you are not as far along in your healing process as you or others would prefer.

Self-care Guidelines

Movement toward your healing can be very draining and exhausting. As different as it might be, seek out people who give you hope for your healing. Permitting yourself to have hope is central to achieving reconciliation.

Realistically, even though you have hope for your healing, you should not expect it to happen overnight. Many bereaved people think that it should and, as a result, experience a loss of self-confidence and self-esteem that leaves them questioning their capacity to heal. If this is the situation for you, keep in mind that you are not alone.

You may find that a helpful procedure is to take inventory of your own timetable expectations for reconciliation. Ask yourself questions like, "Am I expecting myself to heal more quickly than is humanly possible?" "Have I mistakenly given myself a specific time-frame for when I should 'be over' my grief?" Recognize that you may be hindering your own healing by expecting too much of yourself. Take your healing one day at a time. It will ultimately allow you to move toward and rediscover continued meaning in your life.

One valuable way to embrace your healing is to use the journal opportunities in this book. Write your many thoughts and feelings, and you will be amazed at how it helps you embrace your grief. Having experience in writing also can help you see the changes that are taking place in you as you do the work of mourning.

You can't control death or ignore your human need to mourn when it impacts your life. You do have, however, the choice to help yourself heal. Embracing the pain of your grief is probably one of the hardest jobs you will ever do. As you do this work, surround yourself with compassionate, loving people who are willing to "walk with" you.

Personal Self-care Inventory

In the space provided, write out what you are doing or have done to help yourself move toward reconciliation:

CHAPTER

HOW AM
I DOING?

"The body of the person loved is no longer alive, but the memories will live on forever. That part of your whole being that loves him or her is embraced when you allow yourself the privilege of remembering."

A.D.W.

If you are looking for a neatly packaged road map about how to heal in grief, none exists. Everyone's grief journey is unique. No two people will experience it in exactly the same way.

The same thing can be said about how to accomplish your task of mourning, or the outward expression of your grief. What needs to be done in the process of mourning will vary depending upon the individual. Having acknowledged this reality, I want to share with you six central needs of mourning most commonly experienced by bereaved people.

A number of authors have defined models of grief which refer to "stages." As outlined in Chapter II under myths about grief, human beings do not go through orderly and predictable stages of grief that have clear-cut beginnings and endings. Similarly, *the six central needs of mourning I will describe are not orderly and predictable.*

You will probably jump around in a random fashion while working on these six needs of mourning. You will address each need when you are ready to do so. Sometimes you will be working on more than one need at a time. Your awareness of these needs, however, will give you a participative, action-oriented approach to healing in grief as opposed to a perception of grief being something you passively experience.

This concept of needs, or tasks, of mourning, helps eliminate the implication of time limits or orderly, predictable stages. This model of needs is just that—a model. Any model needs to be applied with flexibility and reflect your unique experience and ever-changing needs.

SIX CENTRAL NEEDS

Explore each of the following six central needs of mourning. After each need, you will find questions that will encourage you to write about where you are in addressing these needs.

In summary, the six central needs of mourning are as follows:

1. To experience and express outside of yourself the reality of the death.

2. To tolerate the pain that comes with the work of grief while taking good care of yourself physically, emotionally, and spiritually.

3. To convert your relationship with the person who died from one of presence to memory.

4. To develop a new self-identity based on a life without the person in your life who died.

5. To relate the experience of your loss to a context of meaning.

6. To have an understanding support system available to you in the months and years ahead.

Now, I ask you to explore each one of the needs of mourning individually and relate them to your unique grief journey.

To experience and express outside of yourself the reality of the death.

You can know something in your head, but not in your heart. This is what often happens when someone loved dies. This need involves gently confronting the reality that someone you care about will never come back into your life again.

Regardless of whether the death was sudden or anticipated, acknowledging the full reality of the loss may occur over weeks and months. You may expect him or her to come through the door, to call on the telephone, or touch you. To survive, you may try to push the reality of the death away at times. But to know that someone you love has died is not like flipping a light switch. Nor is embracing this painful reality quick, easy, or efficient.

You may move back and forth between protesting and encountering the reality of the death. You may discover yourself replaying events surrounding the death and confronting memories, both good and bad. This replay is a vital part of this need. It's as if each time you talk it out, the event is a little more real. One moment the reality of the loss may be tolerable; another moment it may be unbearable. Be patient with this need. At times, you may feel like running away and hiding. At other times, you may hope you will awake from a bad dream. As you express what you think and feel outside of yourself, you will be working on this important need.

In the space provided, allow yourself to explore where you see yourself in working on this need. All questions included throughout this chapter are intended as guidelines to aid you in discovering what you are doing with each of the six central needs of mourning.

1. Where do you see yourself in terms of experiencing and expressing outside of yourself the reality of _____'s death?

2. Do you think time is an influence on where you are with this need? Yes _____ No _____ If so, how?

3. Do you respect your need to at times push some of the reality away? Yes _____ No _____ If so, how?

4. Who can you talk with about this need, and where do you see yourself within it?

**To tolerate the pain that comes
with the work of grief while
taking care of yourself physically,
emotionally, and spiritually.**

This need allows you to feel whatever you do about the death. Express your thoughts and feelings with all of their intensity. And, as you encounter your painful new reality, be certain to take good care of yourself physically, emotionally, and spiritually.

Unfortunately, some people around you may not be comfortable with you as you visibly embrace your hurt. Some people will encourage you to "buck up" and get on with life. Yet, your experience has probably already taught you that it's not that easy.

You must have a safe place and time where you can work on this important need. It can be easy to avoid, repress, or deny this need which may include facing confusion, helplessness, and fear following the death of someone loved. In our culture, many people have not learned that hurting is part of healing.

You will probably discover you need to "dose" yourself when experiencing your pain. In other words, you cannot or should not try to do this all at once. Sometimes you may need to distract yourself from the pain of the death, while at other times you create a safe place to move toward it. Working on this need, and all six of these needs, is a process, not an event.

Feeling your pain can sometimes zap you of your energy. When your energy is low, you may be tempted to suppress your grief or even run from it. If you start running and keep running, you may never heal. Remember—with the capacity to love comes the necessity to mourn. Don't become an expert at postponing the inevitable!

If you are a man, be aware that this need may be particularly difficult to address. You may be conditioned to deny pain and encouraged to keep your feelings inside. You may expect yourself to "be strong" and "in control." Yet, despite your efforts of self-control, you may now be experiencing a variety of feelings at an intensity level you never thought possible. To slow down, turn inward, and embrace hurt may be foreign to you. Hopefully, your caring friends will be understanding, patient, and tolerant with you.

Regardless of being male or female, as you encounter your pain, you will need to nurture yourself physically, emotionally, and spiritually. Nurturing yourself physically means such things as maintaining adequate nutrition and getting daily rest and some form of exercise regularly. Emotional needs include such things as a safe place to express whatever you think and feel, and, in general, a nurturing support system that assures you that you are loved. Spiritual needs include knowing it's okay to question your God and having the capacity to embrace "meaning of life" issues.

In the space provided, allow yourself to explore where you see yourself in working on this need.

1. Where do you see yourself in feeling your hurt?

2. Do you think time is an influence on where you are with this need? Yes _____ No _____ If so, how?

3. With whom and how have you shared your feelings of hurt?

4. Are you taking good care of yourself physically, emotionally, and spiritually? Yes _____ No _____ If so, record how for each.

5. If you haven't been talking with anyone about this need, to whom could you talk? _____ How can you establish the relationship to make this possible?

**To convert your relationship
with the person who died
from one of presence to memory.**

Do you have any kind of relationship with someone when they die? Of course. You have a relationship of memory. This need involves allowing and encouraging yourself to pursue that relationship.

Some people may try to take your memories away. Trying to be helpful, they encourage you to pack all the pictures away, tell you to keep busy, or move out of your house. You also may think avoiding memories would be better for you. And why not? You are living in a culture that teaches you that to move away from your grief is best, instead of toward it. Yes, you still have a relationship with the person in your life who died; however, a change must occur from one of presence to one of memory. Memories that are precious, occasional dreams reflecting the significance of the relationship, and living legacies are examples of some of the things that give testimony to a different form of a continued relationship. Your ultimate healing calls out for this new form of relationship that is firmly rooted in memory.

The process of beginning to embrace your memories often begins with the funeral. The ritual offers you an opportunity to remember the person who died and helps to affirm the value of the life that was lived. The memories you embrace during the time of the funeral set the tone for the changed nature of the relationship. Meaningful rituals encourage the expression of cherished memories and allow for both tears and laughter. Memories that were made in love can be embraced with people who shared in your love for the person who died.

Embracing your memories can be a very slow and, at times, painful process that occurs in small steps. Remember— don't try to do all of your work of mourning at once. Go slowly and be patient with yourself.

In a culture where most people don't understand the value and function of memories, you may need help in keeping your precious memories alive. You will need to have people around you who understand your need to share them. The following are a few examples of things you can do to keep memories alive while at the same time embracing the reality that the person has died:

- Talking out or writing out favorite memories you shared with the person who died.

- Giving yourself permission to retain some special keepsakes that belonged to the person who died.

- Displaying pictures of the person who died.

- Visiting places of special significance that stimulate memories of times shared together.

- Reviewing photo albums at special times such as holidays, birthdays, and anniversaries.

Perhaps one of the best ways to embrace memories is through creating a "Memory Book" which contains special photographs you have selected. Organize them, place them in an album, and write out the memories reflected in the photos. This book can then become a valued collection of memories that you can review whenever it seems appropriate.

I need to mention the reality that memories are not always pleasant. If that applies to you, addressing this need can be made even more difficult. To ignore painful or ambivalent memories is to prevent yourself from healing. You will need someone who can nonjudgmentally explore any painful memories with you. If you repress or deny these memories, you risk carrying an underlying sadness or anger into your future years.

In my experience, remembering the past makes hoping for the future possible. Your future will become open to new experiences only to the extent that past memories have been embraced. Hope for your healing means to embrace memories!

In the space provided, allow yourself to explore where you see yourself in working on this need.

1. Where do you see yourself in creating a relationship of memory with the person who died?

2. Do you have people around you who are discouraging you from embracing memories? Yes _____ No _____ Please explain.

3. Did you participate in a funeral ritual that allowed you to have memories? Yes _____ No _____ Please explain.

4. What are examples of things you have done to keep memories of the person who died alive?

5. Were some of the memories painful or ambivalent memories? Yes _____ No _____ If so, what were they?

6. What can you do to continue to work on this need?

**To develop a new self-identity
based on a life without the person
in your life who died.**

Your personal identity or self-perception is the ongoing process of establishing a sense of who you are. Part of your self-identity comes from the relationships you have created with other people. When someone with whom you have a relationship dies, your self-identity, or the way you see yourself, is naturally changed.

You may have gone from being a "wife" or "husband" to a "widow" or "widower." You may have gone from being a "parent" to a "bereaved parent." You may have gone from being an adult child who had "parents" to an "orphan." The way you define yourself and the way society defines you is changed. You may resent working on this need because it makes you confront the reality of the death.

As one woman said, "I used to have a husband and was part of a couple. Now, I'm not only single, but a single parent and a widow . . . I hate that word widow. It makes me sound like a lonely spider. Well, I am lonely, but I'm not a spider."

When you fill out forms, you are often asked to place a check mark in boxes related to how you define yourself. For example, married _____, widowed _____, divorced _____. Every time you have to check one of those boxes, you are confronted with this need of creating a new sense of who you are. At times, you may well automatically find yourself checking the box you have checked for years. If you do, go easy on yourself. Working on this need is a process, not an event.

The death of someone in your life often requires you to take on new roles that were filled by the person who died. Someone still has to take the garbage out, someone still has to buy the groceries, someone still has to balance the checkbook. Your changing identity is confronted every time you do something that used to be done by the person who died. This can be very hard work and, at times, leave you feeling very drained of emotional, physical, and spiritual energy.

You may occasionally feel child-like as you struggle with your changing self-identity. You may feel a temporary heightened dependence on others, feelings of helplessness, frustration, inadequacy, and fearfulness. These feelings can be frightening, but they are actually a natural response to this important need of your mourning.

Remember—do what you need to do in order to survive for awhile as you try to re-anchor yourself. To be dependent on others as you struggle with a changed identity does not make you bad or inferior. Your self-identity has been assaulted. Be compassionate with yourself. Accept the support of those around you who are understanding and supportive as you continue to work on this need.

Whatever you do, don't struggle with your changing identity alone and in isolation. Find someone to "walk with" you as you encounter these changes. As you address this need, be certain to keep other major changes to a minimum if at all possible. Now is not the time for a major move or addition to the house. Your energy is already depleted. Don't deplete it even more by making major changes or taking on too many tasks.

Many people discover that as they work on this need they ultimately come to discover some positive aspects of their changed self-identity. For example, you may develop a confidence in yourself to be independent and survive. You may develop a more caring, kind, and sensitive part of yourself. You may develop an assertive part of your identity that empowers you to go on living while continuing to feel a sense of loss. You may discover a part of your self-identity that has been dormant for years.

In the space provided, allow yourself to explore where you see yourself in working on these needs.

1. Where do you see yourself in working on creating a new sense of who you are?

2. What social and functional role changes are you experiencing as a result of this death?

3. How do you see people treating you differently as a result of your changed identity?

4. Do you ever feel child-like? Yes _____ No _____ If so, how?

5. Do you have a support system that understands your changing identity? Yes _____ No _____ How do they communicate their understanding of your changing identity?

6. What positive aspects have you seen in your changed self-identity?

7. What can you do to continue to work on this need?

To relate the experience of your loss to a context of meaning.

With the death of someone loved, your sense of the meaning and purpose of life is naturally questioned. You may discover yourself searching for meaning in your continued living as you ask "How?" and "Why?" questions.

For example, "How can God let this happen?" or "Why did this happen now?" The death reminds you of your lack of control. It can leave you feeling powerless. You probably will question your philosophy of life and explore religious and spiritual values as you work on this need.

The person who died was a part of you. This death means you mourn a loss not only outside of yourself, but inside yourself. At times, overwhelming sadness and loneliness can constantly be with you. You may feel that when this person died, part of you died with him or her. And now, you are faced with finding some meaning in going on with your life while you at times feel so empty.

This death calls for you to confront your own spirituality. You may doubt your faith and have spiritual conflicts and questions racing through your head and heart. This is normal and part of your journey toward renewed living.

You might feel distant from your God or a Higher Power and question their ultimate existence. You may rage at your God. You are where you are right now! That is all right. Remember—often months of hard work are required to discover the basis for your continued living. But, be assured it can be done, even when you don't have all the answers.

Also keep in mind, a sequential priority occurs of permitting yourself to mourn and question over growing and finding meaning in this death. Some people might say to you early in your grief journey, "Oh, you will grow more from this death and find meaning in ways you didn't know possible." They, however, want you to find meaning immediately after the death. Then they won't have to be with you in the pain of your grief.

Early in your grief, allow yourself to openly mourn without pressuring yourself to have answers to "meaning of life" questions. Move at your own pace as you recognize that allowing yourself to hurt and finding meaning are not "either/or" experiences. More often your need to mourn and find meaning in your continued living will blend into each other, with the former preceding the latter as healing occurs.

At times, feeling like you are in a "holding pattern" in your search for meaning is normal. Before you can grow, you must survive for awhile. Hopefully, you have some people around you who understand your need to be where you are in your search for meaning and who at the same time will be patiently encouraging your continued healing.

In the space provided, allow yourself to explore where you see yourself in working on this need.

1. Where do you see yourself in finding meaning to go on with your life?

2. What were your philosophical, spiritual, and religious beliefs about life and death before this death?

3. Have these beliefs been altered or changed by this death? Yes _____ No _____ Please explain.

4. Do you have any "Why?" and "How?" questions right now? Yes _____ No _____ If so, what are some of these questions?

5. Are you giving yourself permission to question previously held belief systems? Yes _____ No _____ Please explain.

6. Are you punishing yourself in any way for having these questions? Yes _____ No _____ Please explain.

7. Do you ever feel like you are in a "holding pattern" in your search for meaning? Yes _____ No _____ If so, how?

8. What can you do to continue to work on this need?

**To have an understanding
support system available to you
in the months and years ahead.**

The quality and quantity of understanding support you get during your "work of mourning" will have a major influence on your capacity to heal. Because mourning is a process that takes place over time, this support must be available months and years after the death of someone in your life.

Unfortunately, because our society places so much value on the ability to "carry on," "keep your chin up," and "keep busy," many bereaved people are abandoned shortly after the event of the death. "It will be best not to talk about the death," "It's over and done with," and "It's time to get on with your life" are types of comments that still dominate the messages directed to many bereaved people. Obviously, these messages encourage you to deny or repress your grief rather than express it.

If you have people who consider themselves supportive, but who give you these kinds of "mourning avoiding" messages, you will need to find people who can truly be helpful to you. People who see your mourning as something that should be "overcome" instead of experienced will not help you heal.

To be helpful, the people in your support system must appreciate the impact of the death on you. They must understand that in order to heal, you must be allowed and even encouraged to mourn long after the death. And they must encourage you to view mourning not as an enemy to be overcome, but a necessity to be experienced as a result of having loved.

Healing in your grief journey will depend not only on your inner resources, but on your surrounding support system. Your sense of who you are and where you are with your healing process comes, in part, from the care and responses of the people close to you. Your mourning requires support and understanding from the outside—you simply cannot and should not try to do this alone. Drawing on the experiences and encouragement of friends, fellow bereaved persons, or professional counselors is not a weakness. If you lack the capacity to make use of these kinds of resources, your journey will be that much more difficult and overwhelming.

One of the important sayings of The Compassionate Friends, an international organization of bereaved parents, is "You need not walk alone." I might add, "You cannot walk alone." You will probably discover, if you haven't already, that you can benefit from a connectedness that comes from people who also have had a death in their lives. Support groups, where people come together and share the "common bond" of experience, can be invaluable in helping you heal. These groups are usually very patient with you and your grief and understand your need for support long after the event of the death.

You will learn more about support groups and how to create support systems for yourself later in this book. Right now, remind yourself that you deserve and need to have understanding people around you who allow you to feel your grief long after society thinks appropriate.

Unsuspecting waves of your grief can come out of nowhere through a sight, a sound, or a smell. When these waves, called grief attacks or memory embraces, strike you, give yourself permission to talk about it with someone who understands. The reality is right now you do have some special needs that require support, compassion, and nonjudgment from those around you.

In the space provided, allow yourself to explore where you see yourself in working on this need.

1. Where do you see yourself in terms of having an understanding support system at this point in your grief journey?

2. Have you noticed changes in your support system as time has gone by since the death? Yes _____ No _____ If so, what have been some of the changes you have noticed?

3. Who makes up your support system?

4. How are you doing with accepting support from people who try to give it?

5. Do you ever think and feel that you are no longer deserving of support for your mourning? Yes _____ No _____ Please explain.

6. Are you making use of a support group of fellow bereaved persons? Yes _____ No _____ If so, how is this helpful? If not, why not?

7. When you have a "grief attack" or "memory embrace," are people supportive? Yes _____ No _____ Please explain.

8. Are you supportive to yourself at these times? Yes _____
    No _____ If so, how?

9. What can you do to continue to work on this need?

CONCLUDING THOUGHTS ABOUT
THE SIX CENTRAL
NEEDS OF MOURNING

I have outlined the six central needs of mourning to give you some sense of what you can do to help yourself heal. Your needs will continue to change as you permit and encourage yourself to mourn. From time to time, you may want to return to this chapter and review your progress on these needs.

You also might want to develop your own thoughts about what central needs you have encountered as part of your journey. Now, let's turn to some very practical ways to help yourself continue to heal.

TAKING CARE
OF MYSELF

"Your pain is the breaking of the shell that encloses your understanding."

Kahlil Gibran

The title of this chapter does not imply other people in your life do not help you heal in your grief. As emphasized throughout this book, their support in understanding and "walking with" you is essential to your reconciliation. At the same time, you must take responsibility for your own healing.

The following guidelines are just that—only guidelines. Not all suggestions may fit with your needs. Make use of those ideas that make sense to you. You will notice that many of the guidelines have already been referred to in this book. The repetition and summary of some self-help principles is intentional. After completing this book, reread these guidelines occasionally. Reviewing them can help you stay on track as you move toward healing.

TWELVE FREEDOMS OF HEALING IN GRIEF

The following twelve freedoms are intended to help empower you to heal. As you embrace these freedoms, you can discover enormous personal power which results from integrating these principles into your self-care plan. You might want to consider these as "rights" that you have now and of which you need to make use to heal.

1. You have the freedom to realize your grief is unique.

2. You have the freedom to talk about your grief.

3. You have the freedom to expect to feel a multitude of emotions.

4. You have the freedom to allow for numbness.

5. You have the freedom to be tolerant of your physical and emotional limits.

6. You have the freedom to experience grief attacks or memory embraces.

7. You have the freedom to develop a support system.

8. You have the freedom to make use of ritual.

9. You have the freedom to embrace your spirituality.

10. You have the freedom to allow a search for meaning.

11. You have the freedom to treasure your memories.

12. You have the freedom to move toward your grief and heal.

Now I urge you to read closely as I describe in detail each of the Twelve Freedoms of Healing in Grief.

Freedom #1: You have the freedom to realize your grief is unique.

Your grief is unique. No one will grieve in exactly the same way. Your experience will be influenced by a variety of factors: the relationship you had with the person who died; the circumstances surrounding the death; your emotional support system; and your cultural and religious background. As a result, you will grieve in your own special way. Don't try to compare your experience with that of other people. Don't adopt assumptions about just how long your grief should last. Consider taking a "one-day-at-a-time" approach that allows you to grieve at your own pace.

Freedom #2: You have the freedom to talk about your grief.

Express your grief openly. By sharing your grief outside yourself, healing occurs. Ignoring your grief won't make it go away; talking about it often makes you feel better. Allow yourself to speak from your heart, not just your head. Doing so doesn't mean you are losing control or going "crazy." It is a normal part of your grief journey.

Find caring friends and relatives who will listen without judging. Seek out those persons who will "walk with," not "in front of" or "behind" you, in your journey through grief. Avoid persons who are critical or who try to steal your grief from you. They may tell you, "keep your chin up" or "carry on" or "be happy." While these comments may be well-intended, you do not have to accept them. You have a right to express your grief; no one has the right to take it away.

Freedom #3: You have the freedom to expect to feel a multitude of emotions.

Experiencing loss affects your head, heart, and spirit. Consequently, you may experience a variety of emotions as part of your grief work. Confusion, disorganization, fear, guilt, relief, or explosive emotions are just a few of these emotions. Sometimes these emotions will follow each other within a short period of time or they may occur simultaneously.

As strange as some of these emotions seem, they are normal and healthy. Allow yourself to learn from these feelings. And don't be surprised if out of nowhere you suddenly experience surges of grief, even at the most unexpected times. These grief attacks can be frightening and leave you feeling overwhelmed. They are, however, a natural response to the death of someone loved. Find someone who understands your feelings and will allow you to talk about them.

Freedom #4: You have the freedom to allow for numbness.

Feeling dazed or numb when someone dies is often part of your early grief experience. This numbness serves a valuable purpose: it gives your emotions time to catch up with what your mind has told you. This feeling helps create insulation from the reality of the death until you are more able to tolerate what you don't want to believe.

Freedom #5: You have the freedom to be tolerant of your physical and emotional limits.

Your feelings of loss and sadness will probably leave you fatigued. Your ability to think clearly and make decisions may be impaired. And your low-energy level may naturally slow you down. Respect what your body and mind are telling you. Nurture yourself. Get daily rest. Eat balanced meals. Lighten your schedule as much as possible. Caring for yourself doesn't mean feeling sorry for yourself; it means you are using survival skills.

Freedom #6: You have the freedom to experience grief attacks or memory embraces.

Sometimes out of nowhere, you may have a surge of grief come over you. This can be frightening and leave you feeling overwhelmed. These grief attacks or memory embraces are normal and natural. Find someone who understands who will let you talk this out.

Freedom #7: You have the freedom to develop a support system.

Reaching out to others and accepting support is often difficult, particularly when you hurt so much. But the most compassionate self-action you can do at this difficult time is to find a support system of caring friends and relatives who will provide the understanding you need. Find those people who encourage you to be yourself and acknowledge your feelings — both happy and sad.

Freedom #8: You have the freedom to make use of ritual.

The funeral ritual does more than acknowledge the death of someone loved. It helps provide you with the support of caring people. Most importantly, the funeral is a way for you to express your grief outside yourself. If you eliminate this ritual, you often set yourself up to repress your feelings. You also cheat everyone who cares of a chance to pay tribute to someone who was, and always will be, loved.

Freedom #9: You have the freedom to embrace your spirituality.

If faith is a part of your life, express it in ways that seem appropriate to you. Allow yourself to be around people who understand and support your religious beliefs. If you are angry at God because of the death of someone you loved, realize this feeling as a normal part of your grief work. Find someone to talk with who won't be critical of your feelings of hurt and abandonment.

You may hear someone say, "With faith, you don't need to grieve." Don't believe it. Having your personal faith does not insulate you from needing to talk out and explore your thoughts and feelings. To deny your grief is to invite problems that build up inside you. Express your faith, but express your grief as well.

Freedom #10: You have the freedom to allow a search for meaning.

You may find yourself asking, "Why did he or she die?" "Why this way?" "Why now?" This search for meaning is often another normal part of the healing process. Some questions have answers. Some do not. Actually, the healing occurs in the opportunity to pose the questions, not necessarily in answering them. Find a supportive friend who will listen responsively as you search for meaning.

Freedom #11: You have the freedom to treasure your memories.

Memories are one of the best legacies that exist after someone loved dies. Treasure them. Share them with your family and friends. Recognize that your memories may make you laugh or cry.

In either case, they are a lasting part of the relationship that you had with a very special person in your life.

Freedom #12: You have the freedom to move toward your grief and heal.

The capacity to love requires the necessity to grieve when someone loved dies. You cannot heal unless you openly express your grief. Denying your grief will only make it become more confusing and overwhelming. Embrace your grief and heal.

Reconciling your grief will not happen quickly. Remember, grief is a process, not an event. Be patient and tolerant with yourself. Never forget that the death of someone loved changes your life forever. It's not that you won't be happy again. It's simply that you will never be exactly the same as you were before the death.

CHAPTER **IX**

DO I NEED ADDITIONAL HELP?

"To every thing there is a season, and a time to every purpose under the heaven: A time to mourn, and a time to dance;"

Ecclesiastes 3:1,4

Mourning is the normal expression of thoughts and feelings you experience when someone you love dies. It is a necessary, although painful, part of your grief journey. By openly embracing your pain, you will heal from your emotional wounds and reconcile this significant loss in your life in a positive way. Some bereavement therapists refer to this process as "good" grief. It results in growth and constructive change in your life.

Good grief, however, can turn "bad." This situation occurs when normal grief strays off course. Consequently, the work of mourning goes on and on without the bereaved person ever reaching reconciliation. Clinical terms for this type of unfinished grieving include pathological, chronic, inhibited, or delayed. I prefer to call it "complicated grief." Simply stated, complicated grief happens when the common dimensions of grief outlined in Chapter IV become either abnormally intensified or prolonged.

Chapter IX   Do I Need Additional Help?   135

Unfortunately, complicated grief is becoming increasingly pervasive in our society. Why? As a bereaved person, you may not give yourself permission, or receive permission from others, to mourn or outwardly express the conflicting thoughts and feelings experienced when someone you love dies. These feelings become repressed or denied, and while you may find yourself applauded for "being strong" or "doing so well," you are suffering inside.

With no release for your emotions, the grief journey becomes side-tracked; complicated grief often results. You also may experience complicated grief if you have little or no knowledge, or inaccurate knowledge, about experiencing and reconciling the grief process. When someone loved dies, naturally a difficult time occurs. Without an awareness or understanding of what the grief journey may be like or any previous experience with death, you may find yourself set up for a complicated grief experience from the beginning.

The purpose of this chapter is to help you determine if your grief has become complicated. If it has, I encourage you to seek professional help from a trained counselor or grief therapist. To do so is not an admission of failure; it is a positive step in your personal development and an important self-care task.

WHAT CAUSES COMPLICATED GRIEF?

Many factors set the stage for a complicated grief experience. For example, the nature of the death itself may enhance the possibility that your grief might become out-of-step, and as a result, your work of mourning is left uncompleted. For example, was the death of the person you loved sudden or unexpected? Was the way the person died incomprehensible, such as suicide, or were you ambiguous or unsure about how the death actually occurred? Or do you feel in some way responsible for the death? Any one of these factors may trigger complicated grieving.

Your personality also may have an impact on complicating your grief. If you have unresolved feelings or conflicts relating to other losses in your life, or if you have a tendency toward depression, you may be more susceptible. Difficulties in expressing and managing feelings of sadness and anger, extreme dependency on the approval of other people, or a tendency to assume inappropriate levels of responsibility also may complicate your grief journey.

In addition, other contributing factors to complicated grief may relate to your relationship with the person who died. An extreme level of identification, dependency, or an intensely close relationship (to the exclusion of other relationships) with the person who died may be a catalyst. The presence of strong ambivalent feelings or of unresolved conflicts with the deceased also may prohibit you from moving forward in your grief journey. Feelings of guilt related to the life and the death of the person you loved also may have an impact.

Other factors that may complicate your grief journey may include your inability to express feelings related to the loss. For example, you may be unable to accept the high level of emotion which you have experienced as a result of the death. Or perhaps your family, friends, or caregivers fail to validate your intense feelings of grief. In other words, you hurt, and they fail to acknowledge your pain. Other significant losses occurring at the same time, the inability to participate in the grief process due to personal illness, or the lack of access to the usual rituals employed in the expression of grief, such as a funeral, also may provide the impetus for complicated grief.

The excessive use of drugs or alcohol, which suppress your feelings connected with the loss, also may short-circuit what may otherwise be a normal and healthy grief journey. Major religious conflicts that ignore your personal feelings and extreme interpersonal isolation from other people also may be contributing factors to complicating your grief.

While each one of the previously identified factors may be present at some point in your grief journey, their prolonged, extreme, or excessive impact may be a red flag signaling complicated grief. This list of contributing factors is not all-inclusive. Nor do I mean to imply that if any one of these factors is present in your grief journey that you will automatically experience complicated grief. They are outlined simply to alert you to situations that sometimes play a role in complicating the grief process for bereaved persons.

SIGNS OF COMPLICATED GRIEF

How do you know if your grief is complicated? What are the signs that you might need professional help to get you back on track? When "good" grief goes "bad," a few common avoidance behavior patterns may occur. The following behavior patterns sometimes signal the presence of complicated grief.

Postponing Your Grief

In postponing, you may find yourself delaying the expression of your grief in the hope that over time it will go away. Or you may feel that if your grief doesn't vanish, at least a time will come when you feel safer to experience the pain. As a result, you keep pushing your grief aside. Yet the grief builds up within you until a vicious cycle of denial is rooted firmly in place. The consequences of postponing grief are self-destructive, and your grief journey may never end.

Displacing Your Grief

Displacing your grief means taking the expression of your grief away from the loss itself and directing these intense feelings toward other things in your life. For example, you may begin experiencing difficulty at work or in relationships with other people. Unconscious of this behavior pattern, you may become upset or agitated at even the most minor of events. Depression, bitterness, and self-hatred also may occur in this process of projecting the unhappiness that is inside of you onto the outside world.

Replacing Your Grief

If you take the emotions that were invested in the relationship that ended in death and reinvest them prematurely in another relationship, you may be attempting to replace your grief. This action often leads to the complication of your grief journey. As with displacing your grief, you may have little, if any, conscious awareness that you may be avoiding your grief work. This replacement pattern does not only occur in relationships, but in other life activities as well. For example, you may become a compulsive workaholic although you have no prior history of doing so in the past.

Minimizing Your Grief

If you are aware of your feelings of grief but attempt to minimize them through a variety of rationalizations, you may be experiencing complicated grief. You may try to prove to yourself that the loss in your life really doesn't affect you very much. Or you may talk openly about how "well you are doing" and how "your life is back to a normal routine," even though the death may have just occurred. Internally, however, the repressed feelings of grief build within you and emotional strain results. Unfortunately, the more you work to convince yourself that your feelings of grief are overcome, the more emotionally crippled you actually become.

Somaticizing Your Grief

Somaticizing is the clinical expression which describes how you may attempt to convert your feelings of grief into physical symptoms. This converted expression of grief can range from relatively benign minor complaints to a chronic pattern of major ailments that have no organic basis. You may become so completely preoccupied with your physical problems that you have little or no energy to relate to other people or do your work of mourning.

The behavior patterns outlined previously may occur at any time in a healthy grief journey. The persistent and intense demonstration of these behaviors should signal a cause for concern. Anxiety, depression, and actual physical illness result when extreme behavior avoidance patterns go unattended. When these situations occur in your grief journey, no return to happiness, no return to life's normal activities, and no reconciliation can occur.

Respond candidly to the following questions in the space provided below each question. If you answer "yes" to any or all of the questions, you may be wise to seek professional guidance to get you back on track with your normal grief work. However, remember that at any time in your grief journey you may answer "yes" to these questions. When the situations persist, when you feel paralyzed in your grief work, or when you are incapable of living a satisfying existence after the death of someone loved, you need to find a supportive trained professional to help yourself heal.

1. Does your grief interfere with your ability to care for yourself and the capacity to find life meaningful? Yes _____ No _____ If so, please explain.

2. Do you find that you consistently withdraw from people and life in general? Yes _____ No _____ If so, please explain.

3. Do you have physical and emotional symptoms that you do not understand? Yes _____ No _____ If so, please explain.

4. Do you suffer from distorted feelings of anger, guilt, or any other dimension of grief? Yes _____ No _____ If so, please explain.

5. Have you noticed changes in your personality that you cannot seem to control? Yes _____ No _____ If so, please explain.

6. Do you have an internal sense that you are not healing in your grief journey? Yes _____ No _____ If so, please explain.

CONCLUSION

The distinction between normal grief and complicated grief is sometimes difficult to determine. However, in my counseling experience with bereaved persons I have noticed that complicated grief is often a distortion or conversion of the expected mourning process.

If you believe your expression of grief has become complicated as described in this chapter, I urge you to seek help in understanding the dynamics of what you are experiencing. Getting help for yourself is a reflection of your desire to heal in your grief, not a testimony that you are going "crazy."

CHAPTER

WHERE CAN I GET HELP?

"To heal in grief requires outside assistance. When we are bereaved, we need to be compassionate with ourselves as we seek out those who are willing to 'walk with' us in our grief."

A.D.W.

A growing number of individuals, organizations, and self-help groups now specialize in helping bereaved persons. Thankfully, most people no longer believe that anyone has to be "crazy" or "sick" before seeking out supportive counsel. I hope you will allow yourself the opportunity to find the right place to help yourself heal.

This chapter provides some guidelines on finding a professional counselor. Also included is a comprehensive list of organizations and self-help groups that may be of help to you.

HOW TO FIND A COUNSELOR

Finding a good counselor to help with your grief sometimes takes a little doing. The best resource is a recommendation from someone you know and trust. If he or she had a good counseling experience and believes you would work well with this counselor, that may be the best place to start. Even then, however, only you will be able to determine with whom you feel comfortable as a counselor.

If your first attempt at following a friend's suggestion doesn't provide enough information, try more formal methods. The following resources may be helpful:

- A local hospice which may have a counselor on staff who may be available to work with you.

- A self-help bereavement group which usually maintains a list of counselors who specialize in bereavement therapy.

- Your personal physician who can refer you to people trained in bereavement care.

- An information and referral service, such as a crisis intervention center, which maintains referral lists of trained counselors.

- Some funeral homes maintain lists of counselors who focus on bereavement work.

- A hospital, family service agency, and/or mental health clinic usually maintain referral sources.

In making a decision about a counselor who is best for you, your own judgment is essential. Keep in mind, however, that a counselor may have received training in a mental health field, yet may have little or no training in bereavement counseling. Get to know the counselor; you will discover then if she or he has the counseling experience you will find helpful.

DETERMINING IF THIS COUNSELOR IS THE ONE FOR YOU

To determine if you will work well with a counselor, I have included below a list of fifteen questions. While this is not a scientific inventory, my hope is that you will find it helpful. Responses are scored from 0 to 4: 0 = never; 1 = slightly or occasionally; 2 = sometimes or moderately; 3 = a great deal or most of the time; and 4 = markedly or all of the time. Circle the number that most applies after each question.

1. The counselor provides you with a feeling of being understood.

0   1   2   3   4

Empathetic understanding serves as the basis for the work you will do in a counseling relationship. Ask yourself if the counselor has a desire to understand you. Does he or she listen and hear what you think and feel? Without empathy, you will *not* feel understood, and if you do not feel understood, you will probably not trust this person to help you heal. Be aware, though, that understanding is not the same as total agreement. Sometimes, a counselor may understand but disagree.

2. You have a clear understanding of how the counseling experience will help you in terms of your grief and mourning.

0   1   2   3   4

A good counselor can help you understand what the counseling process can do to help you heal. Do not hesitate to ask the counselor how he or she thinks counseling will benefit you. Express your own hopes related to this experience, and see if the counselor agrees that these expectations are realistic. Keep in mind that several sessions may be needed to develop some mutually agreeable counseling goals.

3. The counselor appears genuinely interested and attends to what you are saying.

0   1   2   3   4

In other words, do you feel connected to the counselor? Is he or she alert, sensitive, and caring? On the other hand, does the counselor appears tired, distracted, or overworked? You deserve and need full attention. If you aren't getting focused, genuine attention, look elsewhere for help.

4. Does what the counselor says about your grief and mourning make sense to you?

0   1   2   3   4

This question relates to trusting your instincts. Sad to say, some people are the victims of misinformed counselors who lack training in bereavement counseling. If the counselor makes comments that reflect judgment instead of understanding, you may want to consider another counseling resource. Comments like, "You shouldn't feel that way," or "Have you thought about what you have to be thankful for?" or "You just have to accept it, and get on with life" reflect a judging attitude by the counselor.

5. The counselor encourages you to "teach" him or her about your experience.

0   1   2   3   4

You are the expert about your experience surrounding the death of someone in your life. For the counselor to understand your unique grief journey, he or she must be willing to have you be the teacher about this experience. If the counselor is talking more than you are, odds are that he or she is not allowing you to teach about your individual needs.

6. The counselor helps you explore areas you might want to avoid.

0   1   2   3   4

A helpful counselor will encourage you to talk, think about, and feel certain issues—sometimes uncomfortable issues—that you may want to avoid. Effective counselors often use a skill called "supportive confrontation" to help you participate in the hard work of mourning.

7. The counselor appears to be flexible and open to ideas other than those ideas which reflect only his or her own perspective.

0   1   2   3   4

Openness to different thoughts and ideas is the mark of a good professional. If the counselor appears as an "all-knowing expert" who espouses the only "true answers," you would probably be better helped by someone more flexible and open to your ideas of what is helpful for you.

8. The counselor is willing to explore other sources of support to help you with your grief and mourning.

0   1   2   3   4

While support groups aren't for everyone, many bereaved people find them to be a tremendous help. Your counselor should be willing to help you find additional healing resources. You might ask if he or she is aware of any group experiences or books that have been helpful to other clients.

9. The counseling session is valuable; small talk does not describe your experience.

0   1   2   3   4

While most counseling sessions are characterized by some "warm-up" and social exchanges, counseling is different than small talk. If you talk about everything but your grief and mourning, something is wrong. Either you, the counselor, or both of you may be afraid of encountering the feelings of hurt and loss. A helpful counselor will bridge from warm-up time to more focused ways of helping you work to heal. If you feel like you have a pleasant social experience with your counselor, but don't make progress in your grief work, discuss these feelings with your counselor.

10. The counselor is open and willing to reveal parts of his or her own experience with death that might be helpful to you.

0   1   2   3   4

Some counselors who are distant, never express emotions, or never talk about their own life experiences; they are, however, just not for you. Effective counseling requires a meaningful interchange. The counselor should openly respond to your questions about his or her own experiences with death. While the primary focus should remain your grief work, it is certainly appropriate to ask if your counselor has experienced the death of someone loved in his or her own life. This statement doesn't mean that a counselor must have a multitude of death experiences to be helpful to you. He or she, however, should be willing to respond to your questions.

11. The counselor is interested in talking to other significant people in your life—family, relatives, friends—when it seems that it would be helpful to the counseling process.

0   1   2   3   4

An effective counselor will be interested in how you interact with the people around you. If you, your counselor, or both of you decide to exclude these significant influences, counseling may not be as helpful as it could be.

12. The counselor appears to practice what he or she advocates.

0   1   2   3   4

The helpful counselor is one who will allow himself or herself to mourn when a death occurs. The messages about mourning and practicing good self-care are the same things he or she also has done when doing the work of mourning. Ask your counselor specifically what he or she has found personally helpful.

13. The counselor understands that the concepts of "reconciliation," "accommodation," or "integration" are more helpful than "resolution" or "recovery."

0   1   2   3   4

This statement relates to the counselor's awareness that you are forever changed by the experience of the death of someone loved. If the counselor's goal is to "get you over" or "resolve" your grief, he or she will probably not be helpful. Ultimately, your mutual goals should be to learn to live with your grief while you discover continued meaning in life.

14. The counselor interacts with you as an equal and relates to you in a hopeful, positive way.

0   1   2   3   4

One way to determine that the counselor respects you and considers you as an equal is if you feel comfortable with him or her. If your counselor has an air of superiority and formality, you will probably be better served to find someone else.

15. Your counselor gives you a sense of hope for your healing, while recognizing you are forever changed by this death of someone loved.

0   1   2   3   4

Hope for healing is essential to your ultimate "reconciliation" to the death. No, you won't ever "get over it." Your counselor, however, should be able to help you experience a sense of progress in your work of mourning. While he or she may help you embrace your hurt, you also must have a sense of hope for, and movement toward, your healing.

UNDERSTANDING YOUR SCORE

Again, I remind you that this inventory is not a scientific instrument. Used with caution, however, it can provide you with a sense of whether you are working with a counselor who will be helpful.

Take a moment to total your scores. A score totaling 60 would probably be very unlikely. A score above 45, however, may suggest that the counselor would be a good choice. A score of between 30 to 40 may alert you to the possibility that you should find a more compatible counselor; a score below 30 signals the need to look for another counselor.

In reality, you probably need to meet with a counselor a few times before using this inventory. Sometimes, however, the initial individual-counselor compatibility will be easier to assess, and you will be able to make a much quicker decision as to whether the counselor meets your needs.

COST AND LENGTH OF COUNSELING

The cost of counseling is an important consideration. You will probably discover that costs vary in different regions of the country and from counselor to counselor. The costs generally range between $50 to $100 per session; a session lasts approximately one hour.

Most counselors have a standard fee; however, some individuals will charge less, depending on your ability to pay the full fee. Some counselors also operate on a sliding-scale fee structure based upon your income. Do not hesitate to discuss openly the counselor's fee structure.

Think of the counseling experience as an investment in yourself. While you may have difficulty justifying the expense, what could be more important than your physical, emotional and spiritual well-being? No, you can't drive, eat, or wear the results of counseling. To rediscover continued meaning in your life should be considered one of the best investments you ever made.

Just as fee schedules vary, so do recommendations on the frequency and length of necessary counseling time. This difference usually depends on your unique experience. Some bereaved people only need a few sessions. While others benefit from a longer-term counseling relationship. Discuss this issue openly with your counselor and decide what is best for you.

I often find it helpful to suggest a "time contract" with people I counsel. After an initial consultation, we agree on a certain number of sessions together. Again, the specific number of sessions depends on the individual's unique circumstances. At the conclusion of a pre-established number of sessions, we discuss where the person I am counseling is in his or her grief journey. If the idea of time-limited sessions appeals to you, bring it up to your counselor for discussion.

Regardless of the length of your counseling, doubtfully your sense of progress will occur in an easy, steadily forward direction. The ebb and flow of the healing journey means you may at times feel a lack of constant progress. Be patient with yourself as you continue to remember the person who died, while working to embrace meaning in your continued living. If you feel like sometimes you take two steps backward, then one forward, that is a normal part of the healing experience.

DIRECTORY OF ORGANIZATIONS AND SUPPORT GROUPS

The number of organizations and support groups to help bereaved people are growing at a rapid pace. The following list includes some of the national organizations that may be helpful to you. The list is always changing, so to receive an updated list, write or telephone *Bereavement Magazine.* The editor continually updates organizations and groups for the bereaved. Contact—

Bereavement Magazine
8133 Telegraph Drive
Colorado Springs, CO 80920
(719) 282-1948

To receive a directory of support groups and services available
for **BEREAVED CHILDREN,** contact—

The Dougy Center
P. O. Box 86852
Portland, OR 97286
(503) 775-5683

FOR WIDOWED PERSONS:

Widowed Persons Service
American Association of Retired Persons (AARP)
601 "E" Street N.W.
Washington, DC 20049
(202) 434-2260

THEOS (They Help Each Other Spiritually)
717 Liberty Avenue, Suite 1301
Pittsburgh, PA 15222
(412) 471-7799

National Association for Widowed People
P. O. Box 3564
Springfield, IL 62708

FOR PARENTS WHO HAVE EXPERIENCED
THE DEATH OF A CHILD:

The Compassionate Friends
P. O. Box 3696
Oak Brook, IL 60522
(312) 990-0010

Mothers Against Drunk Driving (MADD)
511 E. John Carpenter Freeway, Suite 700
Irving, TX 75062
(214) 744-MADD = 744-6233

Parents of Murdered Children
100 East Eighth Street, Room B41
Cincinnati, OH 45202
(513) 721-5683

**Sudden Infant Death
Syndrome Alliance**
10500 Little Patuxent Pky, #420
Columbia, MD 21044-3505
(800) 221-SIDS = 221-7437

FOR MISCARRIAGE, STILLBIRTH, ECTOPIC PREGNANCY, AND EARLY INFANT DEATH

SHARE
211 South Third Street
Belleville, IL 62222
(618) 234-2120

FOR MURDER:

National Organization For Victim Assistance
1757 Park Road, NW
Washington, DC 20010
(202) 232-6682

Families of Homicide Victims
2 Lafayette Street
New York, NY 10007

FOR SUICIDE:

American Association of Suicidology
2459 South Ash Street
Denver, CO 80222
(303) 692-0985

FOR TERMINAL ILLNESS:

Make Today Count
P. O. Box 303
Burlington, IA 52601

FOR HOSPICE CARE:

National Hospice Organization
1901 N. Moore St., Suite 901
Arlington, VA 22209
(703) 243-5900

FOR FUNERAL DIRECTORS ASSOCIATION:

National Funeral Directors Association
11121 West Oklahoma Avenue
Milwaukee, WI 53227
(414) 541-2500

FOR AIDS:

AIDS
Action Council
2033 M Street, NW, Suite 802
Washington, DC 20036
(202) 293-2886

POTENTIAL REFERRAL SOURCES FOR COUNSELORS WHO SPECIALIZE IN BEREAVEMENT CARE:

Association for Death Education and Counseling
638 Prospect Avenue
Hartford, CT 06105
(203) 232-4825

American Psychological Association
1200 17th Street N.W.
Washington, DC 20036
(202) 336-5500

National Association of Social Workers
750 1st Street N.E., Suite 7
Washington, DC 20002
(202) 408-8600

**American Association of Marriage
and Family Therapists**
1100 17th Street N.W., 12th Floor
Washington, DC 20036
(202) 452-0109

BEREAVEMENT CAREGIVER TRAINING OPPORTUNITIES:

Center for Loss and Life Transition
3735 Broken Bow Road
Fort Collins, CO 80526
(303) 226-6050

LOCATING ADDITIONAL SUPPORT GROUPS:

National Self-Help Clearinghouse
Graduate School and University Center
Room 620N
City University of New York
33 West 42nd Street
New York, NY 10036
(212) 840-1259

HEALING GUIDELINES FOR SUPPORT GROUPS

"We need not walk alone . . .
We reach out to each other with love and
understanding and with hope . . .
We come together from all walks of life,
from many different circumstances . . .
We need not walk alone!"

Credo, The Compassionate Friends

One of the best tools to assist you in the healing process is participating in a support group. They bring people together who have experienced similar losses. In these groups, each person can share his or her unique journey in a nonthreatening "safe place." Sometimes, people benefit from seeing a counselor as well as joining in a support group. Do what works best for you.

This chapter provides an outline for a support group model based on the content of this book. For the sake of brevity, I have not included all the practical considerations related to starting and operating a support group. For anyone considering the start-up of a support group, I strongly suggest exploring some of the practical questions that naturally evolve when beginning such a process.

Some of the questions to explore are as follows:

- What is the purpose of this group? Will it exist for support, education, social contacts, or therapeutic purposes? What are the differences in these kinds of groups?

- To form the group, should an advisory committee of interested persons in the community be formed? If so, who should serve on this committee?

- What will be the structure of the support group? Will it be "open-ended," meaning that group members can come and go depending on their needs? Or, will it be "closed-ended," in which the group will meet for a specific length of time? Members of this type of support group enter and leave at the same time.

- What bereavement groups currently exist in your community? How are they structured? What kinds of needs do they meet? Would a new support group be a duplication of already existing services or are we working to meet some unmet needs?

- What kind of meeting details must be considered? How many meetings? Where will they be held? How many people will be able to participate in this group? How long will each meeting last?

- Who will facilitate the group? Should the group leader be a lay person or a professional? What is the role of the group leader? Should there be more than one leader?

- What kind of group ground rules should be established? For example, rules such as respecting that each person's grief is unique, what is shared in the group stays there, and that no one will be forced to speak, but everyone will be allowed to express personal thoughts and feelings. Other considerations about the ground rules are: how often do you review them? And, how do you review group expectations?

- What, if any, kind of prescreening will there be for who participates in the group? Is prescreening even important in the first place? Do similarities in the deaths determine who will be included in the group? Or, is finding out how long ago the death occurred in the group member's life important?

- How do you deal with disruptive members? How do you define disruptive? Could your advisory board assist in creating supportive ways to confront disruptive members? Do you have a list of available counseling resources for people who may need additional help?

This list of questions is by no means all-inclusive. I provided the list to give you a sense of the enormous task of starting a group for bereaved persons. Obviously, this task is not for a newly bereaved person. Also, do not try to start a group by yourself. Depending on where you are in your own grief journey, you may discover that you don't have the energy required to get the group started and keep it going. Now many communities have ongoing support groups available that may help meet your needs. Before considering starting a new support group, ask if such a group exists that you could attend.

However, if you want to establish a new support group, an excellent resource is the manual *How to Form Support Groups*, published by Hope For Bereaved, 1342 Lancaster Avenue, Syracuse, New York, 13210. Phone (315) 472-4673.

HEALING GROUP GUIDELINES

When several people read the first draft of this book, they suggested the content would provide a format for a combination education-support group. Accepting this challenge to provide such a structure, I have outlined below a nine-session format. However, be creative and adapt—making changes that you think will best meet the needs of your unique group.

Be aware that this outline is based on a closed-ended support group model. The group meets for nine sessions over an eighteen week format (one meeting every other week). No one can join the group after it begins. For maximum effectiveness, the group should be limited to no more than ten persons.

Preferably, the group should include two facilitators, which will enable them to debrief together after each meeting. The facilitators could be either professional counselors trained in the model outlined in this book, or bereaved persons who have participated in the work of mourning and moved toward reconciliation.

I recommend that prior to implementing this support group an advisory committee of interested persons is formed to address the questions outlined earlier in this chapter. Then, and only then, will you be ready to initiate such a group.

SUPPORT GROUP—MEETING ONE

Introduction/Welcome

The facilitators welcome the participants to the meeting and provide a brief orientation to the purpose of the support group. The introduction and orientation could include comments such as the following:

- *"Welcome. This group will be a combined education-support group. We will use the book, **Understanding Grief: Helping Yourself Heal** as a study guide to help us understand what we might be experiencing."*

- *"Each of our meetings will last 90 minutes; we will meet every other week for 18 weeks. The first half of each meeting will be a discussion based on some content from the book. The second half of each meeting will be left open for group sharing."*

- *"At tonight's meeting, we will get to know each other, distribute the books, and go over our group ground rules. Before we get started, does anyone have any questions or concerns?"*

The facilitator(s) will distribute a printed list of the group ground rules established prior to this first meeting. The group will then review the ground rules and ask questions or share concerns. A sample list of ground rules is outlined below. Your group may wish to make changes or additions to this list.

HEALING GROUP GROUND RULES

1. Each person's grief is unique. While you may share some commonalities in your experiences, no two of you are exactly alike. Consequently, respect and accept both what you share in common with others in the group and what is unique to you.

2. Grief is not a disease. No "quick-fix" exists for what you are feeling. And healing is a process, not an event. Don't set a specific timetable for how long it takes for yourself or others to heal.

3. Feel free to talk about your grief. However, if someone in the group decides to listen without sharing, please respect his or her preference.

4. A difference exists between actively listening to what another person is saying and expressing your own grief. Make every effort not to interrupt when someone else is speaking.

5. Thoughts, feelings and experiences shared in this group will stay in this group. Respect others' right to confidentiality. Do not use the names of fellow participants in discussions outside of the group.

6. Allow each person equal time to express himself or herself so a few people can't monopolize the group's time.

7. Attend each group meeting and be on time. If you decide to leave the group before the completion of

---

this series of meetings, be willing to discuss your
decision with the group.

8. Avoid "advice giving" unless it is specifically requested
by a group member. If advice is not solicited, don't
give it. If a group member poses a question, share
ideas that helped you if you experienced a similar
situation whenever possible. This group is for support,
not therapy.

9. Recognize that thoughts and feelings are neither right
nor wrong. So enter into the thoughts and feelings
of other group members without trying to change
them.

10. Create an atmosphere of willing, invited sharing. If
you feel pressured to talk but don't want to, say
so. Your right to quiet contemplation will be respected
by the group.

Following a review and discussion of the ground rules,
the facilitators can model introducing themselves. If the
facilitators are bereaved persons, they can share something
about the death in their lives and explain why they are attending
the support group. The facilitators can then invite others
to do the same. Acknowledge that participants can say as
little or as much as they like. If a member feels the need
to pause for awhile, the group will understand. Tears need
not be forced, but certainly will be accepted if they occur.
The facilitators should once again remind everyone to not
interrupt when someone else is speaking.

At this first meeting, the sharing process is an important
initial step in creating a supportive, healing group. As people
tell their stories, a powerful bonding usually begins to occur.
Go slowly. Listen; learn; and heal.

At the conclusion of the group sharing, the facilitators will distribute a copy of this resource book to each person. Everyone is asked to read Chapters I and II before the next meeting. Obviously, group members should be encouraged to come prepared to discuss the material and their reactions to what they have read. Members also should be asked not to read ahead in the book. Reading the text should be a group experience. So go slowly, and go together as a unit. Lastly, each person should be asked to bring to the next meeting a picture of the person in their life who died.

SUPPORT GROUP—MEETING TWO

Explanation of Content

I suggest that you start this meeting by having members share the pictures of the persons in their lives who died. They might also tell something about the picture and why they picked this particular one to share with the group. Members might explore qualities about the person that this picture portrays. This activity assists the group members in getting to know those persons who have died. It also helps the bereaved person begin the long and difficult process of simply acknowledging the death while embracing memories.

Following the picture sharing, the facilitators will lead a discussion of the reaction to the content of Chapters I and II. Approximately the second half of this and every following session should be used for open-ended discussion.

Chapter I—Potential Discussion Questions

The facilitators should explore the following questions with support group members (Members may wish to use the space provided to explore their responses):

1. What do you think of being an "active participant" in your own healing?

2. Has anyone been relating to you as a "patient"? Yes _____ No _____ If so, what does this feel like for you?

3. Dr. Wolfelt cited a quote by C. S. Lewis which says, "An odd by-product of my loss is that I'm aware of being an embarrassment to everyone I meet . . . Perhaps the bereaved ought to be isolated in special settlements like lepers." How does this quote relate to you? Do you feel shame or embarrassment about your grief? Yes _____ No _____ Please explain.

4. Has anyone negated or even dismissed your need to mourn? Yes ____ No ____ If so, what does it feel like to you?

5. Chapter I discusses the need to make a personal commitment to healing. Does this make sense? Yes ____ No ____ Are you ready to make use of this support group as a "safe place" to mourn?

Chapter II—Potential Discussion Questions

Suggestion. The facilitators simply can state the myths and encourage an open discussion surrounding them. Following or as part of this discussion, these questions might be explored:

1. Have you been the victim of this myth? Yes _____
   No _____ Please explain.

2. What persons around you have perpetuated this myth?

3. How will your new awareness of this myth influence your grief journey?

Homework. For the next meeting, each participant should read Chapter III and bring something reflecting the unique relationship with the person who died. Examples include a poem composed about the relationship, a special song or piece of music, an item belonging to the person who died, or whatever will help fellow group participants learn something about the unique relationship with the person who died.

SUPPORT GROUP—MEETING THREE

Explanation of Content

Try starting this meeting with group members sharing what they have brought that reflects the relationship with the person who died. This activity allows for and emphasizes how each person's relationship with the person who died is unique. During this activity, there may be tears, laughter, or quiet silences. The facilitators should help try to make the group a safe place for the wide variety of responses to this and any other activity.

Following this period of sharing, the facilitators will lead a discussion of the reaction to the content of Chapter III.

Chapter III—Potential Discussion Questions

Suggestion. A helpful procedure often is for the facilitators to write on a chalkboard or flip chart the ten factors outlined in the chapter. The group can then refer to them and explore the various questions provided after each factor. Time will probably not allow participants to explore each question. Facilitators can use their judgment on how to process these questions. Depending on the group size, if six to ten participants, a suggestion is to break into smaller groups of three to five each so participants can discuss the factors more fully.

Homework. Participants should read Chapter IV prior to the next meeting and make a collage depicting the various feelings they have encountered in their grief journeys. Instructions for the collage are as follows: (1) Get a large poster board, glue, and lots of old magazines. (2) Look through the magazines for images (often faces) reflecting feelings that you associate with your grief experience. (3) Be creative. Draw your own images or use pictures you have of yourself. (4) Put together a collection of images that depicts the feelings, thoughts, or experiences that are a part of your encounter with grief. No one will be graded for artistic abilities, and no right or wrong or good or bad collage exists.

SUPPORT GROUP—MEETING FOUR

Explanation of Content

Have participants share their collages with the group. The facilitators may want to go first to serve as a model. As participants show their collages, they should be encouraged to express why the pictures reflect their grief encounters. The rest of the group is not required to interpret or judge the collage. Participants will bring their own personal meanings to this activity. Allow for questions for clarification, not interpretation. This activity allows and encourages participants to identify some of the feelings experienced through the grief process. Participants may express similar feelings helping to create a sense of "walking together." The result is that participants will probably begin to feel less alone in their grief journeys.

Following the collage sharing, the facilitators will lead a discussion of the reaction to the content of Chapter IV of the book.

Chapter IV—Potential Discussion Questions

Suggestion. Generally, a helpful procedure will be to write on a chalkboard or flip chart the various dimensions outlined in Chapter IV. The group can refer to them and explore how the dimensions fit with the experiences of participants in the group.

Facilitators should explore the following questions with support group members:

1. Which of these dimensions have been a part of your grief experience so far?

2. In discussing disorganization and confusion, Dr. Wolfelt describes the "going crazy syndrome." Have you experienced this feeling? Yes _____ No _____ If so, what did it feel like for you?

3. Has your body let you know it is under stress? Yes _____ No _____ If so, how? What are you doing to rest and take care of yourself?

4. Have any of the explosive emotions (anger, hate, blame, terror, resentment, rage, and jealousy) been a part of your grief experience so far? Yes _____ No _____ If so, what has this been like for you?

5. Have guilt, regret, or self-blame been a part of your grief experience? Yes _____ No _____ If so, how?

6. What are some times that bring about deep feelings of loss, emptiness, and sadness? How do you respond to these feelings? How can this support group help you during these difficult times?

7. Have you experienced a sense of relief as described in this chapter? Yes _____ No _____ If so, could you help us learn what that has been like for you?

This chapter may generate numerous questions and create a discussion that could last for hours. The facilitators will have to use their own judgment of how to manage this discussion. Usually, participants will guide the facilitators to areas about which they need to talk.

Homework. Before the next meeting, each participant should read Chapters V and VI and select one of the areas outlined in Chapter V that most relates to his or her grief experience. In the next session, those members, who feel comfortable doing so, will be encouraged to teach other participants about this part of their grief journey.

SUPPORT GROUP—MEETING FIVE

Explanation of Content

A possible way to start this meeting is to have the facilitators write the subtitles of Chapter V on a chalkboard or flip chart. The group can refer to them as each person shares how one of the areas most fits with his or her experience. Again, group members should not be forced to talk, but invited to talk, so other participants can listen and learn.

After group members share how these aspects of grief relate to them personally, the facilitators should lead a discussion of the general reaction to the content of Chapter V. I have found that it is a good idea for one of the facilitators to model talking about Loss of Intimacy and Sexuality. Some participants may be afraid to acknowledge the loss of sexual intimacy. This subject, however, is one that many bereaved people need to talk about. Don't force this conversation. On the other hand, don't avoid it either.

After the discussion questions for Chapter V, have group members to share their views of Chapter VI. Then lead a discussion of questions for Chapter VI.

Chapter V—Potential Discussion Questions

1. Which of these aspects of grief have been a part of your experience so far?

2. Do you remember the section on "transitional objects"? Yes _____ No _____ What are some examples of belongings that link you to the person who died? Has anyone tried to distance you from these objects? Yes _____ No _____ If so, how did you feel?

3. What did you think of the section on "suicidal thoughts"? What is the difference between passive thoughts of suicide and active thoughts?

   Note: If anyone acknowledges active suicidal thoughts, assist that person in getting professional help *immediately.* Do not minimize the seriousness of suicidal thoughts as "normal." You may save a life!

4. What are some examples of "memory embraces"? What is it like for you when you experience one?

5. What have been your experiences with dreams? What are these experiences like for you? What do your dreams mean to you?

6. Have you ever had a mystical experience? Yes _____
   No _____ If so, could you share it with the group?

7. What are your experiences with drugs and alcohol? Do
   you suspect that you may have a drug or alcohol problem?

   Note: If anyone needs help in this area, refer the person
   to a drug and alcohol counselor. Keep in mind,
   however, denial is often a component of a drug
   and alcohol abuse or dependency problem.

   This chapter may generate numerous questions and create
discussion that could last for hours. Again, the facilitators
should use their discretion about where to take this discussion.
Participants also may teach the facilitators where the course
of the discussion should lead.

Chapter VI—Potential Discussion Questions

1. What does the concept of "reconciliation" mean to you? Does it make more sense to you than terms like "resolution" or "recovery"? Yes _____ No _____ If so, why?

2. Has anyone told you that you should "be over your grief" by now? Yes _____ No _____ If so, what has that been like for you?

3. Which of the criteria for "reconciliation" have you experienced? Are you being compassionate with yourself by not expecting yourself to heal more quickly than is humanly possible? Yes _____ No _____ Please explain.

4. Are you finding that the journalizing process is helpful to you in your healing process? Yes _____ No _____ If so, how?

Homework. Before the next meeting, each participant should read Chapter VII and select one of the six central needs of mourning to talk about with the group. Facilitators should remind group members that all of the needs are important to healing; however, each participant should focus on one need to discuss at the next meeting. It could be a need that the participant is currently working on or that needs to be addressed in the future. The questions that follow the description of each need in Chapter VII will help participants teach the group about their experiences.

SUPPORT GROUP—MEETING SIX

Explanation of Content

Try starting this meeting with the facilitators writing the six central needs of mourning on a chalk board or flip chart. Each member can refer to it as he or she talks about these central needs with the group. The questions following each need outlined in this chapter may help participants teach each other about how they perceive themselves to be working on these needs. Again, invite but don't force anyone to talk. The other participants will listen and learn.

Following each person's opportunity to talk about one of the six central needs of mourning, the facilitators will lead any additional discussion. If one or more of the six needs has not been talked about, the facilitators should initiate discussion to do so. Particular attention is to be given to the sixth need, *To have an understanding support system available in the months and years ahead.* Discussion about this need can once again emphasize that healing in grief is a process, not an event. Even after this group concludes, members will need continued support in doing the work of mourning.

Chapter VII—Potential Discussion Questions

Facilitators should use the questions following the description of each need to stimulate a discussion. Also, be creative. Think of some discussion questions that are not outlined in this chapter.

Reemphasize that these six central needs are not orderly or predictable. An awareness of them, however, can help each person have an action-oriented approach to healing in grief. Allow the second part of the session for open-ended discussion.

Homework. Ask each participant to read Chapter VIII before the next meeting. Request that each participant make a Memory Book and bring it to the next meeting. In this Memory Book, each participant will place objects such as pictures, letters, poetry, written tributes, artwork, or anything else that reflects memories of the person who died. Some people may choose to use a chronology of pictures depicting different life-phases of the person who died. Emphasize that no one will be graded for artistic ability. Everyone will have an opportunity to show his or her Memory Book and talk about it at the next meeting.

SUPPORT GROUP—MEETING SEVEN

Explanation of Content

Try starting this meeting by having each person share his or her Memory Book with the group. The purpose of this exercise is to help create meaningful ways of remembering the person who has died. In addition, a Memory Book helps address the third central need of mourning: *To convert the relationship with the person who died from one of presence to one of memory.* These Memory Books are valuable because they create a memorial in honor of the person who has died. While assembling the book often brings tears of sadness, it will also often bring sounds of laughter as memories surface.

Following this activity, facilitators can pass out a list of the "Twelve Freedoms of Healing In Grief" from Chapter VIII. A helpful tool is to have a group member read aloud the information outlined in the book after each Freedom. Something powerful occurs when this information is read aloud in a group setting. It becomes almost like the group's *Bill of Rights.* Possibly, a different group member can read each one of the Twelve Freedoms. Either pause for discussion after each one or read all twelve consecutively and then begin discussion.

Homework. Ask each participant to read Chapter IX before the next meeting. Also, ask each person to contact someone before the next meeting who also has been bereaved but is not a member of the support group. This person may be someone familiar or a complete stranger. This homework encourages participants to reach out either by letter, telephone, or in person, and let someone know they care. Request that each member of the group write a brief note of what he or she did and how the bereaved person responded. Encourage each participant to talk about this experience at the next meeting.

SUPPORT GROUP—MEETING EIGHT

Explanation of Content

Try starting this meeting by having each person discuss his or her experience of reaching out to another bereaved person. Encourage group members to express feelings and concerns. How did the bereaved person respond? Finally process what the group learned by doing this activity. Its purpose is to rehearse and reinforce the need to mutually reach out to one another. In learning how to support others, hopefully each participant will be even more willing and able to ask for future help.

Following this activity, the facilitators should lead a discussion of the group's reaction to the content of Chapter IX.

Chapter IX—Potential Discussion Questions

1. Does your grief interfere with your ability to care for yourself and the capacity to find life meaningful? Yes _____ No _____ If so, please explain.

2. Do you find that you consistently withdraw from people and life in general? Yes _____ No _____ If so, please explain.

3. Do you have physical and emotional symptoms that you do not understand? Yes _____ No _____ If so, please explain.

4. Do you suffer from distorted feelings of anger, guilt, or any other dimension of grief? Yes _____ No _____ If so, please explain.

5. Have you noticed changes in your personality that you cannot seem to control? Yes _____ No _____ If so, please explain.

6. Do you have an internal sense that you are not healing in your grief journey? Yes _____ No _____ If so, please explain.

Homework. Ask each participant to read Chapter X before the next meeting. Also, request that each person come prepared to talk about what he or she has gained from this group experience.

SUPPORT GROUP—MEETING NINE

Explanation of Content

Begin this session by acknowledging that it is the final meeting of the support group. Changing the format of this meeting from past meetings, the facilitators should begin by asking if anyone has questions about Chapter X. The discussion should focus on identifying additional sources of support to assist in the continued work of mourning. This chapter is self-explanatory and may not generate too much discussion. Some members may be seeing an individual counselor and want to talk about this experience.

Use the remainder of this group meeting for closure. Sitting in a circle, encourage each person to express what he or she feels was gained from this group experience. Ask everyone to give a "verbal gift" to a fellow participant. A verbal gift is a positive comment a member has observed about another participant during the support group. It might be something the person shared that helped you in the healing process.

Each person is encouraged, but not forced, to participate in this discussion.

The facilitators should then thank everyone for attending the support group and reinforce that they hope each member has been helped in his or her healing journey.

HELPING A FRIEND
IN GRIEF

This Chapter is to identify how you can help a friend who has experienced the death of someone loved. You want to help, but you are not sure how to go about it. This chapter will guide you in ways to turn your cares and concerns into positive actions.

Or you may want to share this chapter with a friend to help him or her understand how he or she can help you in your grief.

GUIDELINES FOR HELPING

Listen with Your Heart

Helping begins with your ability to be an active listener. Your physical presence and desire to listen without judging are critical helping tools. Don't worry so much about what you will say. Just concentrate on listening to the words that are being shared with you.

Your friend may relate the same story about the death over and over again. Listen attentively each time. Realize that this repetition is part of your friend's healing process. Simply listen and understand.

Be Compassionate

Give your friend permission to express his or her feelings without fear of criticism. Learn from your friend; don't instruct or set expectations about how he or she should respond. Never say, "I know just how you feel." You don't. Think about your helper role as someone who "walks with," not "behind" or "in front of," the one who is bereaved.

Allow your friend to experience all the hurt, sorrow, and pain that he or she is feeling at the time. Enter into your friend's feelings, but never try to take them away. And recognize that tears are a natural and appropriate expression of the pain associated with the loss.

Avoid Cliches

Words, particularly cliches, can be extremely painful for a grieving friend. Cliches are trite comments often intended to diminish the loss by providing simple solutions to difficult realities. Comments like "You are holding up so well," "Time will heal all wounds," "Think of all you still have to be thankful for," or "Just be happy that he's out of his pain" are not constructive. Instead, they hurt and make a friend's journey through grief more difficult.

Understand the Uniqueness of Grief

Keep in mind that your friend's grief is unique. No one will respond to the death of someone loved in exactly the same way. While it may be possible to talk about similar phases shared by grieving people, everyone is different and shaped by experiences in his or her life.

Because the grief experience is unique, be patient. The process of grief takes a long time; so allow your friend to proceed at his or her own pace. Don't force your own timetable to healing. Don't criticize what you believe is inappropriate behavior. And while you should create opportunities for personal interaction, don't force the situation if your grieving friend resists.

Offer Practical Help

Preparing food, washing clothes, cleaning the house, or answering the telephone are just a few of the practical ways of showing that you care. And, just as with your presence, this support is needed at the time of the death and in the weeks and months ahead.

Make Contact

Your presence at the funeral is important. As a ritual, the funeral provides an opportunity for you to express your love and concern at this time of need. As you pay tribute to a life that is now passed, you have a chance to support grieving friends and family. At the funeral, a touch of your hand, a look in your eye, or even a hug often communicates more than any words could ever say.

Don't just attend the funeral then disappear. Remain available afterwards as well. Remember your grieving friend may need you more in the days or weeks after the funeral than at the time of the death. A brief visit or a telephone call in the days that follow are usually appreciated.

Write a Personal Note

Sympathy cards express your concern, but no substitute for your personal written words exists. What do you say? Share a favorite memory of the person who died. Relate the special qualities that you valued about him or her. These words will often be a loving gift to your grieving friend, words that will be reread and remembered for years.

Use the name of the person who has died either in your personal note or when you talk to your friend. Hearing that name can be comforting, and it confirms that you have not forgotten this important person who was so much a part of your friend's life.

Be Aware of Holidays and Anniversaries

Your friend may have a difficult time during special occasions like holidays and anniversaries. These events emphasize the absence of the person who has died. Respect this pain as a natural extension of the grief process. Learn from it. And, most importantly, never try to take away the hurt.

Your friend and the family of the one who has died sometimes create special traditions surrounding these events. Your role? Perhaps you can help organize such a remembrance or attend one if you are invited.

Understand the Importance of the Loss

Remember that the death of someone loved is a shattering experience. As a result of this death, your friend's life is under reconstruction. Considering the significance of the loss, be gentle and compassionate in all of your helping efforts.

SUMMARY

While these guidelines will be helpful, recognize that helping a grieving friend will not be an easy task. You may have to give more concern, time, and love than you ever knew you had. But this effort will be more than worth it.

By "walking with" your friend in grief, you are giving one of life's most precious gifts—yourself.

CHAPTER

A FINAL WORD

"Time is relative to the emotional forces during any given period of life. In a time of tragedy the rapid movement of your emotions may make it seem that you have lived more, endured more and learned more in a few days than in months of ordinary living."

Edgar N. Jackson

In the beginning of this book, I wrote that "When someone we love dies, our capacity for love dictates our necessity to mourn." Yes, to heal you must mourn. But, to mourn, you also must have people around you who are understanding and supportive as you embrace the pain of your loss.

Perhaps the most compassionate self-action to remember at this time in your life is to find a support system of caring friends to provide the listening ear and open heart you need. Find someone who encourages you to be yourself and acknowledges your many thoughts and feelings. Be self-loving. Be patient with yourself. Waves of grief will continue to ebb and flow in your life; just as the love you have for the person who died lives on.

As it should be, thoughts, feelings, and behaviors that result from the death of someone loved are impossible to ignore. As you continue to experience how grief has changed your life, be open to the new directions your life now is taking. Grief may change your priorities, and I urge you to make decisions about your life you may never have considered before. Listen to your head. Listen to your heart. Listen to your inner voice.

As you embrace your grief, you can and will find that the pain softens. Once again you will be able to enjoy life. You will rediscover that you care for and about others. And yes, you will laugh and smile again.

The experience of grief is powerful. So is your ability to help yourself heal. In doing the work of grieving, you are continuing toward a renewed sense of meaning and purpose in your life. I hope this book has helped to create a safe place for you to embrace your pain as you move toward your healing.

Right now, take a moment to close your eyes; open your heart; and remember the smile of the person in your life who has died.

INDEX

INDEX

Guilt 63-7
    feelings 63
    joy syndrome 65
    magical thinking 65
    relief syndrome 64
    survival 64

H

Hate 59-63
Headaches 56
Healing 130-4
    See freedoms of healing
Heart palpitations 56
Help
    counselor 143-50
    determining if needed 135-42
    offering practical 185
    organizations 151-5
    sources 143-55
Helping
    friend in grief 183-6
    guidelines for 183-6
Helplessness 86-7
Holidays
    grief occasions 83-4
    help a friend during 185-6

I

Illness
    identifying symptoms of 85-6
    physical symptoms of 85-6
Intimacy
    loss of 92-3
Inventory
    See self inventory
    See self-care inventory

J

Jealousy 59-63

L

Lewis, C.S. 1
Limits
    physical and emotional 132

Listen with your heart 183
Loss 67-71
Love
    ability to 1-5

M

Meaning
    search for 77-8, 133-4
Memory
    embraces 82-3, 132
    treasure of 134
Minimize grief 139
Mood
    sudden changes 84-5
Mourn
    necessity to 1-5
Mourning 104-28
    See needs of mourning
    definition 1, 8
    progress toward 103-28
    work of 17
Muscle
    aches and pains 56
Myths
    about grief 7-16
    about mourning 7-16

N

Nausea 56
Needs of mourning 104-28
    central six 104-5
    convert relationship to memory 110-4
    develop a new self-identity 114-8
    experience and express outside of self 105-7
    relate the experience to a context of meaning 119-22
    tolerate the pain 107-10
    understanding support system 123-7
Noise
    sensitivity 56
Note
    write a person in grief 185
Numbness 45-9, 132

O

Objects
    transitional 79-80
Obsessive review 76-7
Organizations
    directory of 151-5

P

Pain
    moving toward 5
    tolerate 107-10
Panic 53-5
Participant
    active 2
Personality
    long standing factors 64
    of the person who died 28-30
    your unique 25-8
Postponement
    grief 138
Powerlessness 86-7
Progress
    toward mourning 103-28

Q

Queasiness 56

R

Rage 59-63
Reality of the death 105-7
Reconciliation 13
    as healing 97-102
    criteria for 99-100
Regret 63-7
Relationship
    to one of memory 110-4
    with the person who died
      18-20
Release 72
Relief 72
Religious background 32-5
Replacement
    grief 138-9

Resentment 59-63
Ritual 133
Rules
    healing group 161-2
Ruminating 76-7

S

Sadness 67-71
Searching 49-52
Self inventory
    anxiety, panic, and fear 54
    disorganization, confusion,
      searching, and yearning 51
    explosive emotions 61
    guilt and regret 65-6
    loss, emptiness, and sadness 70
    own unique healing process 100
    physiological changes 57
    relief and release 72-3
    shock, denial, numbness, and
      disbelief 47
Self-blame
    feelings 63
Self-care guidelines 66, 73
    anxiety, panic, and fear 54
    disorganization, confusion,
      searching, and yearning 52
    explosive emotions 62
    guilt and regret 66
    hearing 101
    loss, emptiness and sadness
      70-1
    physiological changes 57-9
    release and relief 73
    shock, denial, numbness, and
      disbelief 48
Self-care inventory
    anxiety, panic, and fear 55
    disorganization, confusion,
      searching, and yearning
      52-3
    explosive emotions 62-3
    guilt and regret 67
    loss, emptiness, and sadness 71
    move toward reconciliation 102
    psysiological changes 59
    relief and release 73

Self-focus 95-6
Self-identity 114-8
Sex, biological 38-9
Sexuality
    loss of 92-3
Shock 45-9
Shortness of breath 56
Sleep
    trouble with 55
Sobbing 88-9
Somaticize grief 139
Sources
    help 143-55
    organizations 151-55
Spirituality 133
Spiritual background 32-5
Stresses
    in your life 35-7
Suicide
    thoughts 81
Support groups
    closed-ended 159
    directory of 151-5
    guidelines 157-81
    meeting eight guidelines
        178-81
    meeting five guidelines 171-6
    meeting four guidelines 168-71
    meeting nine guidelines 181
    meeting one guidelines 160-3
    meeting seven guidelines 177-8
    meeting six guidelines 176-7
    meeting three guidelines 167-8

    meeting two guidelines 163-7
    meetings one through nine
        160-81
    questions in starting 157-9
Support system 22-5, 123-7, 132-3

T

Tears 5, 14-5
    See crying
Tension 56
Terror 59-63
Time distortion 75-6

U

Understand the importance of loss
    186
Understand uniqueness of grief 184

W

Weight
    loss or gain 56
Write
    person in grief 185

Y

Yearning 49-52

ABOUT THE
THE
AUTHOR

ABOUT THE AUTHOR

Dr. Alan D. Wolfelt talks like he writes—from the heart as well as the head! He has become known to thousands of people who find his gift to teach a true inspiration.

He is the founder and director of the Center for Loss and Life Transition in Fort Collins, Colorado. A respected author, educator, and clinical thanatologist, Alan's books include *Death and Grief: A Guide for Clergy, Helping Children Cope with Grief,* and *Interpersonal Skills Training: A Handbook for Funeral Home Staffs.*

Dr. Wolfelt serves as an educational consultant to hospices, hospitals, schools, universities, funeral homes, and a variety of other agencies. The editor of the "Children and Grief" department of *Bereavement* magazine, he also writes a regular feature article titled "Thanatologist's Corner" for the journal *Thanatos.*

Alan is known for his outstanding educational contributions in both adult and childhood grief. His compassion and love for life are felt when one is in his presence.

To inquire about the Center's Training Opportunities and to write to Dr. Wolfelt, contact the Center for Loss and Life Transition, 3735 Broken Bow Road, Fort Collins, Colorado, 80526. Phone (303) 226-6050.

TRAINING OPPORTUNITIES
FOR FACILITATORS

Dr. Wolfelt and the Center for Loss and Life Transition offer regularly scheduled training opportunities for persons interested in becoming certified group facilitators based on the content of this book.

To receive information about this training opportunity, write or phone:

The Center for Loss and Life Transition
3735 Broken Bow Road
Fort Collins, Colorado 80526
(303) 226-6050